Galen Brookens

ODD SOCKS & OTHER SHORT PIECES

ODD SOCKS &

OTHER SHORT PIECES

Nancy Johnson

With Illustrations by Susan Behling

RAMSHORN PUBLISHING CO.

Fremont, Michigan 49412

Illustrations by Susan Behling

Copyright © 1986 by Nancy Johnson

Publisher: Ramshorn Publishing Company
P.O. Box 263
Fremont, Michigan 49412

Library of Congress Catalog Card Number: 85-62548

ISBN 0-9615478

TO HARTMAN,
WHO KNOWS WHO HE IS
NO MATTER WHAT I CALL HIM,
WITH LOVE.

Contents

ACKNOWLEDGEMENTS	xi
FOREWORD	xiii
1. TIME AND THE TELEPHONE	1
2. BEARING IT	5
3. ODD SOCKS	9
4. CRUISING	13
5. THE FINE ART OF CONVERSATION	15
6. BODY LANGUAGE	19
7. WHAT'S IN A NAME?	23
8. THE HIRSUTE MALE	27
9. DEEP POUCH	31
10. BEHIND IN TIME	35
11. ON BICYCLES	37
12. A NUMBER OF LAKES	41
13. HEAD TABLE	45
14. THE WAVE	49

CONTENTS

15. DO THEY RUN IN THE FAMILY?	55
16. SHOPPING BLUES	57
17. SORRY I ASKED	61
18. AH, THOSE SENTIMENTAL TEARS!	65
19. HOME FOR THE HOLIDAYS	69
20. SELF IMPROVEMENT	73
21. DIET EVERYONE?	77
22. ON AN EMPTY NEST	81
23. OFF TO THE RALLY	85
24. THE ABSENT MIND	89
25. HIDDEN MESSAGE	93
26. LONG TERM STORAGE	97
27. YARD SALE	101
28. A RITE OF PASSAGE	105
29. A LEGENDARY TREE	109
30. TACKY TACKY	115
31. A STATE OF PERFECT REPAIR	119
32. RADIO ALARM	123

33. SHIFTING	127
34. CHOCO... CHOCO... CHOCOLATE	131
35. THE ART OF PHOTOGRAPHY	137
36. ON ICE	141
37. BURNT CRISP	145
38. SMALL TOWN	147
39. AGE IS A MATTER OF TIME	151

Acknowledgements

The pieces included in this book originally appeared in somewhat different form in the Times-Indicator published in Fremont, Michigan. "Odd Socks" and several other pieces--I've lost track of which ones--also appeared in The Grand Rapids Press.

I want to express my gratitude to Susan Behling whose drawings capture so well the spirit I wanted to convey in this book.

I am grateful to J. J. Lamberts, a one-time Fremont boy, a former editor of the Fremont Times-Indicator, professor of English at Arizona State University in Tempe, Arizona, and writer, for his kindness, patience, and perception in editing the manuscript. He graciously gave me the benefit of his editorial skill, his teaching experience, and his talent to make ODD SOCKS... a better book.

I am grateful, too, for the friends, neighbors, acquaintances, and total strangers who have told me that something I wrote sounded a familiar note in their lives. Their comments mean more than they know.

To my children for their good humored tolerance and help, and to my husband for his encouragement, unfailing support, and constant love, my heartfelt thanks. Without them, I would not be me.

Foreword

                    I should be able to tell you something about this book and about me that would make it all hang together. But then, perhaps the book doesn't hang together any better than my life. Most of my days seem to be made up of short pieces, none of them matching any more often than the odd socks forever turning up in the wash.

  I don't want to give the impression that I lead a disconnected life. The mates to those odd socks and to the short pieces of my life are around here somewhere, and I'll run across them yet. They can't have gone far. I still grow where I was planted, live and write in the same small town where I was born, and where my father and my father's father lived.

  My husband, with whom I have lived happily for many years, complains good-naturedly about appearing in my pieces thinly veiled. But we are still married to each other, which is a biographical note worthy of mention these days. And he has not yet pulled the plug on my typewriter--the most effective form of protest. So I write on, searching for the pieces that match up.

  When I meet someone on the street in our small town, a thousand common memories inform our greeting, "How are you?" The owner of the hardware store went to school with me. The woman waiting at the traffic light shared my hospital room and maternal joy when we both had babies more than thirty years ago—and yet just last month, it seems. The butcher's wife was a sister of my mother's hired girl. We have smiled and said "Hello", and little more than that, for years. But each time we greet, a memory floats into mind and adds a piece of pleasure to a day.

I saw one such friend in the grocery store a while ago. "When are you going to put those pieces you write for the paper in a book?" she asked. "I meant to save the last one, but Fred used the newspaper for cleaning fish before I had a chance to cut it out."

Such has been the fate of most of the pieces I've written. They end up wrapped around the garbage, or tied in bundles for sale to Rag & Metal at half a cent a pound. Not that I mind. One must be good for something in this world.

Still, it was as good a reason as any for producing a book, and I told my friend with the fish-cleaning husband that I'd get right to work.

N.J.

Fremont, Michigan
1985

1. Time and the Telephone

"Tempera mutantur, nos et mutamur in ellis," or, Times change and we change with them, the ancient Latin saying goes.

At this point in time--an American saying dating back to Watergate--we are changing with the Bell telephone company. For one thing, we are getting used to the new Fremont Area Telephone directory which turned up in our mailboxes last month. It is an impressive 8 x 11 inches, with 100 yellow pages, 92 pages of names and numbers from A to Z, and 24 pages of Customer Guide which tells us about the services Michigan Bell provides and how to do business with them. Call them. Of course. Big city stuff, that.

The new phone book is a far cry from the 6 x 9 directory we've used for years. It is still a farther cry from the 6 page edition of the phone book in which I looked up my first telephone number.

`A far cry´, by the way, was mankind's first long distance call.

A person didn't really need a number to make a phone call back in the 1930's when we used the 6-page directory. All I needed to do, as I recall, was turn the crank that rang the bell and tell "Central" I wanted to talk to "my daddy".

Central spent her time upstairs over the Crandall & Ensing Furniture Store. I often sat on the step in front of my father's office and watched her through the window across the street, pulling out and putting in plugs. I assumed she had her switchboard in that window so she could look up and down Main Street and keep track of everything that was going on in town. Maybe someone would call me sometime while I was sitting on that step and she would lean out of the window and tell me—with a far cry—that I was wanted on the phone. Hers was, I thought at the time, wonderfully interesting work.

Hartman, a little boy in town back then whom I absolutely hated—or pretended to—and whom I later married, had an Aunt Mary who was "Central" over in Clifford. Her switchboard took up two-thirds of the space in her tiny living room, and when she didn't have anything else to do, she'd listen in. You weren't supposed to, but you could get on the party line and have eight-way conversations. At this point in time, eight-way conversations are all right. They call them conference calls.

But Aunt Mary was Central before time had points. In those days, time marched on, went by, came, passed, and waited for no man. It also changed, as it does today, bringing us back to the new phone book and the 24 page Customer Guide which makes rather interesting reading and calling, if you're into that sort of thing. Which, the other day, I was.

For instance, the Guide tells you where to pay your phone bill if you want to pay in person. In Fremont, the Guide states on page 15, pay at Chris' Drugs. Even Michigan Bell can't keep up with all the changes of late. There hasn't been a Chris' Drugs in Fremont for several years.

So I called my Service Representative who has,

in changing times now past, taken Central's place. She said that bills could be paid in Fremont at the Country Squire Pharmacy, or at the Old State Bank of Detroit.

"Of Detroit?" I said.

"Yes," she replied. "That's what it says here. Old State Bank of Detroit at 2 West Main Street in Fremont."

I wonder if the Old State Bank of Fremont knows that.

I called the Service Representative again to request a couple of out of town telephone directories, free of charge. In the time it takes to place a phone call, "she" had changed into a "he". "You don't call those cities very often," he observed, evidently looking at my record on a computer screen.

"I don't?" I said, surprised. It seemed to me from my phone bill that I called those cities several times a week. But that may not be often according to Bell standards. In these changing times, everything is relative. I promised to do better in the future, and a few days later the directories turned up in the mail.

I then called, several times,--the last time under an assumed number to keep Bell from thinking me a pest-- the Let's Talk Customer Information Center number listed on page 1 of the Customer Guide section of the new directory.

The Information Center serves Michigan, Indiana, and Ohio. It is manned or womanned-- as the case may be--by eight Bell Service Representatives and two supervisors from 8 AM to 11 PM every day. They handle about 300 calls a day from the tri-state area.

Most of the callers, my Representative--whose name was Linda--told me, ask about the rental or purchase of telephones, the relative costs, the repair service, etc. But the Representatives are trained to discuss anything about telephone communication and the changes occurring because of the divestiture resulting from the government anti-trust actions in 1974 and 1976.

In preparation for their day on the telephone, Linda and her cohorts, latter day "Centrals", are required to read four daily newspapers: The New York Times, The Wall Street Journal, and the two Detroit papers. This week Linda, who wondered what I would be saying about the telephone company, will be reading one weekly paper as well.

I think it must be interesting work.

2. Bearing It

Every year in Michigan we have the great deer hunting season. Last year a record 210,000 deer were taken out of the woods. Dead, you may be sure. Some 700,000 hunters, nearly ten times the population of Saginaw, are trying their luck in Michigan this year. The deer kill, according to the best estimates, may reach a record level in this state.

Cooking venison I don't mind, but I can't stand cooking bear meat. Several years ago, before I knew about bear, a kindly neighbor expressed his thoughtfulness by giving us a bear roast. I accepted the gift gratefully. When you consider the cost of the gun, the ammunition, the hunting gear, the hours spent planning the trip, the camp food, transportation, days away from work, money the little-woman-left-at-home spends on frivolities while the hunter is tramping the forest, the license, and miscellaneous costs-- easily the biggest item on the expense list--game meat is not cheap. I imagine the five pound bear roast the neighbor gave us was worth not a cent less than $400. And it had to be cooked.

As many times as I have prepared venison, squirrel, rabbit, pheasant, and partridge, I had never cooked bear. In my innocence I thought the strange aroma which rose out of the kettle soon after I put the roast on the stove was just the way bear was supposed to smell. I decided it would be prudent to put the bear in the portable electric roaster and finish cooking it in the back kitchen.

"Back kitchen" is an expression left over from my childhood when we lived in a house where there used to be a woodburning cookstove. The woodburning cookstove was gone long before I came on the scene, but its place in the back kitchen and the back kitchen itself were still there. Early settlers who cooked bear as a matter of course, I reasoned, must have always cooked it in the back kitchen where bad smells wouldn't bother people.

Our house didn't have a back kitchen, but it did have a back room where the children left their muddy boots. Whenever I got the portable electric roaster out and cooked something in the back room, I called the room the back kitchen. Dual-purpose rooms are not only popular but necessary in the kind of homes we build today.

Wood burning has come back into vogue, and so most people can imagine what a woodburning cookstove is, but there is a whole generation of young people who will not remember the portable electric roaster. A portable electric roaster is a free-standing rectangular oven. It weighs a ton. It was a popular appliance in the '50's before wide ovens and microwave ovens came on the market. It is about as portable as a 48" TV.

Nevertheless, I was driven by the smell of that bear roast to haul the roaster out of the basement and plug it into the nearest electrical outlet. As the meat kept on bubbling in the back kitchen, I couldn't help but notice that the strange odor had begun to seep around the edges of the firmly closed door.

It was late in the afternoon. One by one the children came home from school, left their muddy boots next to the portable electric roaster and sought out their mother. "What stinks?" they asked.

"Supper," I said.

One by one they called their grandma, wangled an invitation, packed their bags, and left for the night.

I found an extension cord and with a display of the superhuman strength often granted us in moments of dire need, moved the roaster and the nauseating bear roast out to the porch. Combine a paper mill in full production, a large poultry house on a July afternoon, and a pile of burning tires and you will get an idea of how that bear roast smelled. And the smell was beginning to fan out over town.

Never had I been personally responsible for such a public nuisance before. It troubled me to see people roll up their car windows as they drove past the house.

Evening approached. The family provider--Hartman--left the office and followed the trail of the scent to its source. "Something has just come up," he said, holding his hand over his mouth. "I'm going hunting just as soon as I can get my gear in the car."

I'm used to his goings and comings and he is used to mine. Our marriage is the better for it. Kahlil Gibran was right when he wrote those lovely words about marriage in THE PROPHET: "...let there be spaces in your togetherness/ And let the winds of the heavens dance between you.../ And stand together yet not too near together:/ For the pillars of the temple stand apart..."

In this case, however, it was an ill wind that danced between the pillars of our temple and I refused to bear it alone.

"What can I do with the bear?" I asked.

"Dump it," he said.

"A rotten suggestion," I replied sweetly. The trash pick-up was another three days away the bear could explode by then. And of course I couldn't bury it; it was the sort of thing the dog would dig up and roll in.

Fortunately for the temple of our marriage, a brilliant thought came to both of us at the same time. Without a word we each siezed an end of the portable electric roaster and hassled it into the trunk of the car. Moments later it was on its way to deer camp, stunning citizens along the route.

Soon a fresh breeze sprang up. I opened all the windows in the house and went out to shop for frivolities.

I don't know what Hartman did with the bear and the roaster. He came back from deer camp empty handed that year.

And I didn't ask.

3. Odd Socks

The past half hour I spent sorting socks. Nine black ones, seven green ones, three brown ones, and two olive drab ones with the elastic tops long gone. The one matched pair.

For all the years I've been keeping house, socks seem to come not in even but in odd numbers. The olive drab socks are the only ones that proceed through the laundry as a pair. And nobody in the family admits wearing them.

Not only mystified, but upset by the proliferation of odd socks, the sock wearers in the family look to me for an answer. They maintain that odd socks cannot be. Where do the other socks go? They take off not one, but two socks every night, they say, and put two socks in the laundry. It is not the kind of claim I feel I need to check up on, but I have my doubts.

As they cast about for some explanation of the single sock syndrome, they have gone on to charge me with dropping socks with holes in them into the wastebasket instead of darning them. But if they would look in their sock drawers they would know how wrong they are. Actually, I put the socks with holes in them back in the drawers, holes and all.

The socks wearers of the family have gone so far as to charge me with deliberately dropping socks down behind the washing machine where they will be forever lost. This is a nasty slander. Only last Christmas when the washing machine decided to take a holiday on its own, I seized the opportunity to sweep behind it. There were buttons, some pennies and dimes, a peanut butter sandwich,--at least I assumed it was a peanut butter sandwich; that is the only kind of sandwich we've had around here since the kids learned to talk—at least a pound of dust, and only one sock. And that lone sock didn't match any of the odd socks that were stockpiled at the bottom of the clothes basket.

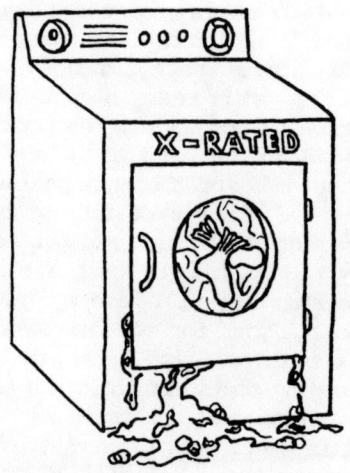

We can photograph the secret locations of hidden missiles from outer space, and calculate the value of pi to hundreds of decimal places, but do our finest minds know what happens to those missing socks?

A number of theories have been set forth, of course. One of the most engaging suggestions is that the socks are not missing at all. Instead they have mated within the innards of the Maytag so that every pair dropped into the warm suds comes out a threesome.

Friends of mine who firmly believe this tell me that the chances are 20 to 1 that in another 25 years one of the offspring will match up with another. Unfortunately that doesn't seem to be happening at our house. But--just in case we manage to get a match one of these happy days-- I haven't thrown out an odd sock in 19 years.

So much for all of that. My own guess is that our town has a ring of one-legged bandits who go around pinching socks--one at a time. Till the law nabs them, my hoard of odd socks will probably continue to grow.

4. Cruising

Cruising, as any parent knows, is a time-honored custom among young American drivers everywhere. The requirements for cruising are: a valid driver's license and the use of a car. Any car. The purpose of the activity is social: you drive around to see who you can see.

When I was a teenager in Fremont, we used to cruise down Main Street, around the high school, past the park at Fremont Lake and as far as Hesperia on a Sunday night.

In recent years I have cruised again as each child in the family entered the driver-training stage and had to practice driving with an adult in the car.

The experience has shown me that Fremont cruising patterns hardly change at all. Kids still cruise down Main Street, drive around the high school, circle city park, and turn right at the Mini-Mart, as they have for years. They also cruise past their friends' houses and honk twice. We used to do that too. There may be subtle variations in cruising etiquette from one generation of kids to the next, but the basic cruising patterns do not change. I found cruising with young people rather fun, but our 15-going-on-16 year old learning driver of a year or two ago didn't find it fun to have me along. It was hard, he complained, to act cool at the wheel of a car with your mother in the front seat telling you what to do.

Cool? We didn't know cool back in my teenage cruising days.

He thought my behavior as a passenger in a cruising car left something to be desired. I called out the car window to my own friends, and waved at people he didn't even know. It was embarrassing, he said, as bad as showing up at school with galoshes on. Couldn't I just ride along and be invisible?

I tried. Time passed and he passed through that stage. Now he views with tolerant amusement the discomfort of his younger sibling who must cruise these next few months with Mother who's not cool in the front seat.

But parents can learn too. My friends who see me cruising with our learning driver this time around will see me looking neither right nor left. It's not that I am frozen stiff with fear, it's just that I've learned "cool".

5. The Fine Art of Conversation

I found a book on Eskimos on my father's bookshelf a while ago. He's been collecting books on all sorts of subjects for seventy years and his library is a literary treasure house. The book on Eskimos, out of print now, was written by a man who'd lived among them in the early '30's, It was full of fascinating Eskimo lore. The trouble is, Eskimos are hard to bring into a conversation so it isn't the sort of knowledge one can put to very good use.

The other day, for instance, I was lingering over lunch with some friends at Foghorn--it's The Foghorn Country Club, actually, but we call it Foghorn for short--and tried to add to the general conversation about food with a description of 'giviak'.

"First you flense a seal," I said. My friends looked puzzled so I told them how to do it. "You just free the skin from the seal's body with a sharp knife and pull the body out through the mouth opening. This leaves a sealskin bag lined with blubber." My friend Betty turned a bit green and pushed her plate away. But then, she has a sensitive stomach.

"Then you catch some auks," I continued. "They're little birds that you catch on the wing like flies. About twenty of them are supposed to nicely fill a medium size sealskin bag. All you need to do to prepare them is braid their wings together and stuff them into the flensed sealskin, feathers and all. No refrigeration necessary. You just put the stuffed sealkins in a safe place outdoors somewhere and cover it with stones so the animals can't get at it. In about six weeks or so the blubber from the sealskin seeps into the birds, cures the meat and makes them almost heavenly to eat. Or so they say."

"It's so hard to find the ingredients for those exotic dishes," Jane murmured politely. Nobody else seemed interested enough to write down the recipe. There was a brief silence and then the conversation turned to children.

"Eskimo babies are carried against their mother's bare backs underneath their parkas," I said. "The babies don't wear diapers and what happens just has to be tolerated."

Jane and Mag glanced toward the next table to see if we were being overheard, then quickly changed the subject. Everyone began talking about the floor plan of the Smithson's new house.

"Eskimos live in one room houses," I ventured during the first lull in the conversation. "Everyone in the family and all their overnight guests sleep together on a platform that runs along the back of the house."

This time they prattled on about Jo's remodelling project as if I hadn't spoken at all. I decided to make one more effort to bring anthropology into the conversational gambit before giving up to our more prosaic interests.

"It's really true that they loan their wives to friends, neighbors and honored guests," I said apropos of nothing. "But it's supposed to be a very useful custom in Eskimo culture. They stick

THE FINE ART OF CONVERSATION 17

strictly to certain rules of etiquette that govern the practice."

At last I'd struck a topic that caught their interest. Everyone , including the people at the next table, was listening open-mouthed.

"Stop!" Mag cried, interrupting me not two minutes after I'd finally gotten the floor. "Don't say another word. I haven't got a program for Book Club yet. Save your Eskimos and do the book for us there."

Mag is my father's other daughter and she knew where I'd gotten all that Eskimo stuff.

6. Body Language

BODY LANGUAGE by Julius Fast was a pop-psychology best seller which introduced the decade of the seventies. It dealt with the raised eyebrow, lifted lip, shrugged shoulder, and other signals people use to speak without words. "It is important to realize," the author said, "that body language is different in different cultures."

I know that statement is true, and I wish I'd known it before I went to Puerto Rico. It might have saved us from what almost became an international incident.

It happened at the airport in San Juan. We were people-watching as we waited for an overdue plane, and my eye grazed the Van Dyke beard on a dark little man.

Apparently he caught a signal I never intended to send, for he walked to the bench where Hartman and I were sitting, knelt on the floor, and with a flourish, bent low and kissed my foot.

No one had ever kissed my foot before. Not even my closest friends. It completely took my breath away.

While I sat stunned by the wonder of it all, the dark little man sat down beside me and tried to strike up a conversation. In Spanish, I think. Or Swahili.

It doesn't matter. Hartman, who was several times larger than the dark little man, was not stunned. He leaned forward, glared, and said in plain English, "Get lost."

He had a suggestion for me too. "Why didn't you kick him in the eye while he was down there?"

I had read very little--absolutely nothing, in fact-- about the etiquette of foot kissing, but I was sure a kick in the eye would not be listed among the appropriate responses. I assumed what Julius Fast in BODY LANGUAGE might term a posture of indifference, which was probably not listed among appropriate responses either.

In the meantime, the dark little man, who was on my right, moved still closer, began to speak English, and was joined by another dark little man with a Van Dyke beard. Evidently a twin.

I hate scenes. But I could tell by the body language of the man on my left, Hartman, that there was certainly going to be one. His nostrils flared, his eyes narrowed, and a pulse in his forehead throbbed. He leaned in front of me and stared, long and hard, at the two dark little men.

My posture of indifference vanished as I jumped to my feet and tugged at Hartman's arm. He shrugged me off, plainly stating without words that I was no longer of any consequence in the matter.

Fortunately his body language was clear in any culture. The dark little man who had kissed my foot looked down at his hands. "Hokay, Senor," he said, and went away with his twin.

7. What's in a Name?

The question of what to call the new parents-in-law has plagued newlyweds for generations. So far as I know, it is one problem those pillars of wisdom--Ann Landers, Billy Graham, and Heloise--have never addressed.

Logically speaking, this should not be a problem at all, but who is logical anymore? For some reason the names 'Mom' and 'Dad' when brought forth to address the new spouse's parents, seem to stick in the throat. That's no one's fault; that's just the way it is.

So what else do you call them? Mr. and Mrs. Vanbrotmarkle--provided that is their name of course--seems too formal, especially to a bride who has just become Mrs. Vanbrotmarkle herself. And to call them by their given names--Englebert and Lucrezia, for instance--seems, in many cases, a bit too chummy.

According to an informal survey conducted at a recent party, better than eight out of ten of the couples interviewed had solved the problem when they were first married by calling their parents-in-law nothing at all. This has its disadvantages, especially when the mother-in-law has planted herself right in front of the salt and doesn't know enough to pass it.

The problem of what to call the in-laws goes a long way to explain why the birth of the first child is an occasion for such joy for everyone concerned. At last something can be found to call the hitherto nameless ones. Nana and Bobba will do, or Mimi and Goopa. Or, if all else fails, there is really nothing wrong with Grandma and Grandpa.

One out of ten of those interviewed in the survey stated that as newly-weds they called their in-laws "You", with heavy emphasis on the Y. Still others, perhaps wishing to be more specific, said "Hey, You."

Three of those polled simply said they called in-laws by their first names when they were newly married. Two percent managed to come out with "Mom" and "Dad", and a few used a miscellaneous assortment of expressions that are perhaps better not made public.

There were also some ways of handling the situation revealed by the survey. One mother-in-law said she wrote to her future son-in-law before the wedding to suggest that he could call her either Mother Vanbrotmarkle or by her given name. It was all the same to her, she told him, either name would do, just so she was called something.

This seemed to me an excellent solution to the problem, and I decided to follow her example when I became a mother-in-law.

However, as the date of the wedding of our first off-spring to marry drew near, I was seeing my prospective daughter-in-law several times a day. It hardly seemed appropriate to write her a letter; she might have thought I was mad at her. So I let it go. As luck would have it, she joined the number of newlyweds who use given names.

The problem may be around well into the 21st century, but a word of advice to newlyweds is in order anyway.

If you don't know what to call your new parents-in-law, don't fret. Twenty-odd years ago, before your spouse was born, your in-laws probably didn't know what to call Gaga and Tooty either.

8. The Hirsute Male

A psychologist from the University of Chicago has conducted an experiment on the psychology of mustaches and beards. He published his findings in "Psychology Today".

A mustache or a beard, according to the results of his experiment, heighten a man's sexual magnetism in the eyes of women and make him appear more dignified and mature in the eyes of other men. Whether they admit it or not.

People tend to stand farther away from a man with facial hair than they would if the same man were clean shaven.

Only lack of interest prevents me from launching an experiment of my own on beardedness, but I have a hunch that every man and woman in the country has a strong opinion on the subject and feels compelled, for some unknown reason, to express that opinion.

You stand a better chance of walking down Fremont's Main Street unremarked in a Scotsman's kilt than you do with new grown hair on your face. Provided of course you are male.

I know this is true because my husband Hartman once grew a mustache.

Now one would think that if he chose to decorate his upper lip with hair, it would be a matter of profound indifference to the citizens at large. But this is not true.

At this particular time in the history of the human race, and in this particular place, the public looks upon a mustache or a beard as a disturbance of the peace. They feel they have a moral obligation to pass judgment on those whose bristly adornments intrude upon tranquility.

Clean shaven, Hartman was just another person in the crowd. But sporting a new mustache, he set off a chain reaction which rippled through a room. Perfect strangers—only strangers are perfect; the rest of us have flaws and we love each other regardless—volunteered to tell him how to trim it, and where and if to put the curls. Mere acquaintances came up to say he looked like George Peppard, or else the Old Man of the Sea.

Some people regarded his mustache as an act of aggression and told him angrily to shave it off, while others—pretty young women, mostly—stood in line for an experimental kiss.

In spite of the young women, I liked him with a mustache. But he finally shaved it off. He got tired of wearing a conversation piece.

It was six long weeks before someone noticed that it was gone.

9. Deep Pouch

Heloise, a columnist who specializes in practical advice on how to get through the nitty gritty of life, has suggested that women carry twist ties in their purses so that when a button pops off a coat or a pair of eyeglasses come apart, they can make a quick repair no matter how far they are from home.

It seems like a good piece of advice and since I need help getting through life's nitty gritty, I'd like to take the suggestion. I may already have a twist tie in my purse for such emergencies; goodness knows I have everything else. All I need to do is find it.

That is the difficulty. I am sure I spend a third of my life looking for something in my purse. The purse I carry at present is actually a pouch. A key pocket near the top of the pouch is too small to hold a set of keys but is the perfect size for a twist tie. If I run a twist tie into my finger while I rummage for keys at the bottom of the pouch purse, I can put it into the key pocket. I could also squeeze a Band-Aid into the key pocket if I should happen to find an extra while looking for one to stanch the flow of blood from my wounded finger.

The pouch purse I am using now is not the only purse I've ever had. The other purses I've had are at this moment resting under a layer of dust on the top shelf of my closet. I don't like any of them any better than "the pouch", but they are too good to throw away.

Some of the purses stashed on the top shelf are too small to put anything in. One of them is so hard to open it probably still contains whatever was in it the last time I used it. Another has a saber-toothed zipper guaranteed to scratch the hand that feeds it. Still another has three dividers which empty into a common trough at the bottom. Whoever designed that number just didn't think things through.

The purse I carried before I took up "the pouch" had thirteen compartments. This is true. I never did figure out what all those compartments were designed for, but I managed to fill them up the very first day. The rest of the time I carried that purse I spent trying to remember which compartment to look in for what.

That experience prompted me to buy the present purse with only one side pocket which turned out to be too small for keys and a single huge pouch. I had been compartmentalized so long I failed to anticipate the jumble my possessions would get into at the bottom of a pouch.

In order to get organized, then, I bought two small cotton bags. Into one of the bags I put everything pertaining to the body: comb, paper handkerchiefs--known as Kleenex to most of us-- aspirin, lipstick, nail file, dark glasses, and much more. Into the other cotton bag went everything pertaining to the mind: pens, shopping lists, notices from the library about overdue books, slips of paper containing uplifting thoughts to calm me when I can't find anything in my purse, and the small black leather notebook which contains my brain. It occurs to me that one should date shopping lists. Twice now, I've shopped off last week's list. It was impossible to decide whether credit cards, driver's license, family pictures, and money had to do with body or mind, so I have taken to carrying a billfold containing the above items in a coat pocket. It is a good idea to store the billfold in a coat pocket because I stand a better chance of finding it before the stores close.

Actually, all I need to carry when I venture out of the house is a piece of tissue for my nose, a couple of tacky dollar bills in case of a financial emergency, and the black leather notebook.

The problem is that the black leather notebook is too big to fit into any pocket ever attached to anything a woman is likely to wear. And if I didn't have that notebook with me at all times I wouldn't be able to tell you that the Japanese invented nose tissues and have used them since before 1637 when an Englishman first reported they blew their noses on paper handkerchiefs called hanagami. Kleenex, the first American paper handkerchief, appeared in 1924.

So. I guess I'm doomed to carry a purse of some sort the rest of my life. It is the only thing which will contain that black leather notebook. If I didn't have that with me, how could I tell you these things?

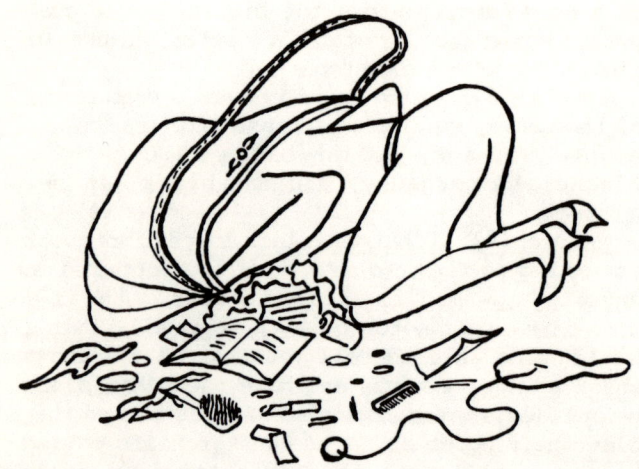

10. Behind in Time

A number of years ago, as I was dressing for my wedding, my mother took me aside and gave me her first and only advice to the bride: "Read TIME MAGAZINE," she said. "At least then you'll have something to talk about."

But reading TIME hasn't been the certain road to social success Mother said it would be. Whenever I interject something I read in TIME into the conversation, people look startled and a pall falls over the gathering.

I've thought of three possible reasons which might explain why this happens: TIME comes to the house every week; I am a slow reader; these have been a very busy 25 years.

I'm gaining, however. Last night I finished the final issue of 1965.

A friend once suggested I switch to another news magazine because I probably wouldn't live long enough to fall so far behind in my reading again. But as I see it, that would be the coward's way out. And those who live in the same small town all their lives are not cowards. They may be other things equally reprehensible, as their fellow townspersons know all too well, but they are not cowardly.

TIME isn't the only reading I've fallen behind on. I'm one of the main contributors to the Overdue Book Fines at the Fremont Public Library. Overdue Book Fines amount to enough money each year to pay the library electric bill.

Besides that, they stopped publishing the weekly "Saturday Evening Post" 10 years ago, but I can't stop reading it until sometime next month.

Then there are the "New Yorker," "Sports Illustrated," three daily papers--don't ask me why--and monthly publications like "National Geographic," "Smithsonian," "Arizona Highways," Popular Mechanics," ...oh, why go on?

I once read about two Brooklyn eccentrics who had only narrow passageways between the stacks of newspapers and magazines piled floor to ceiling in their house. What's so eccentric about that?

11. On Bicycles

I haven't seen any recent statistics on the number of bicycle riders extant—I looked that word up and it means 'still in existance', which is a good way to put it when you consider the peril they put themselves in on the road—but I imagine that by now there must be millions of them. Ten-speed bicycles are ubiquitous. Thieves won't even steal your three-speed bikes anymore.

As a motorist, I don't know how long I will be able to cope with all these bikes. It's my nerves, you know. On a recent drive in and around town I ran into no fewer than 22 bicyclists. Loosely speaking, of course.

Bicyclists were going down the street five abreast. When a car came near they either ignored it or peeled off in all directions like kids caught cooning melons in the dark. Or they chose to come at you up the wrong side of the road, wobbling scarily as they tried to stare you down. Sometimes they'd sashay back and forth, run stop signs, or dart across your path as you approached. To put it mildly, it wracked the nerves.

Age makes no difference in the way bicyclists behave these days. Young or old, they are as unpredictable as squirrels. Don't they know they should obey the rules of the road, go single file, keep to the far right, stop at stop signs, proceed at a steady pace, just as cars do?

No, they do not.

On the other hand, as a bicyclist myself, the motorists on the streets and roads reduce me to a mass of quivering nerves. Bicycles, like cars, have the right of way on a through street. Yet cars pull out in front of me as if I'm not there. Or drivers will turn left across my lane. Once I ran my bike into a driver turning left. It served him right, but it hurt me more than it did him.

Or the driver blasts his horn in my left ear and brushes past my fender baskets at 70 miles an hour. Motorists should lightly touch the horn button when they are two car lengths behind a bicyclists, slow down and wait to pass, giving the cyclist a reasonable section of the road. Not to mention other common courtesies. Don't motorists know that?

No, they do not.

The Newaygo County Bicycle Association promotes good biking, maps for bicycle trails, races, bike hikes. Those involved in their activities, I assume, know how to ride safely. And one presumes that when they are in the driver's seat of a car, they know the proper manners too.

But there are other cyclists like me who merely bike for pleasure or for exercise. And there are motorists who never ride a bike at all, of course. I'd like to see the NCBA pound car and cycle etiquette in to both of us.

And I'd like to see them do it soon, before there are no more bicyclists extant.

12. A Number of Lakes

Occasionally I have the pleasure of introducing Fremont and its environs to visitors from out of town. On such occasions, I am rather pleased with our little corner of the universe. It is especially nice in the spring. And summer, fall, and winter.

But there is one thing I have always apologized for when the visitors' tour of the city took us out Ramshorn Road. Four things, actually: First, Second, Third, and Fourth Lakes.

Do not misunderstand. The lakes themselves do not embarrass me. Far from it. They are beautiful little lakes. Their shapes alone, nestled as they are among gentle hills, are enough to inspire an artist. They are alive, cold, and full of many kinds of fish. My young nephew caught an 18" bass in one of them last year, and a 17" bass this year. The woods and meadows surrounding the four lakes teem with wild life. And they are situated right on the edge of our town, within walking distance. How lucky can we be?

But the names of those lakes do not do them justice. Or so I used to think. Whatever was the man who named them thinking of? First, second, Third, Fourth. What kind of names are those?

Those lakes are jewels of nature where you can spot a ruffed grouse, pheasant, partridge, raccoon, or possum. Mink and wild turkey pass through, and wood ducks live there. And deer. Why not name them something which would evoke such images?

Especially in springtime the lakes deserve better names. Trillium, cowslips, and purple and yellow violets bloom along their shores. There are adder's tongue, dutchman's britches, jack-in-the-pulpits--a hundred of them in one small area last year--skunk cabbages, and may apples galore.

There are watersnakes in abundance too, and, more to my taste, puff balls as large as cantaloupes, morels and meadow mushrooms in season, and even the choice and delicious slippery jack.

Slippery jack. Now there is a name. Whoever named the slippery jack mushroom had imagination. Class.

The person who named the streets in Baldwin, Michigan, forty miles north of Fremont, had imagination too. Baldwin streets have truly inspired names: Joy, Nirvana, Righteous, Kindness, Paradise, Creation, Miracle, Patience, Unity, and Wilderness Way. Those names are wonderful. But First Lake? Second, Third, and Fourth? No way.

Or so I used to think. Then one day I held forth on this subject in the presence of my nephew, 12 years old, the one who catches bass and knows those lakes as no on else around here does.

"I like the way those lakes are named," he said. "The names tell you what you need toknow, like which lake you are on."

Straightforward names, he meant, without pretense. He has a good point. The next time I take someone past one of those lakes and they ask what lake that is, I´ll say, "Second," in a good loud voice. And I´ll not apologize.

13. Head Table

Summer has arrived at last and the rounds of banquets, meetings, and receptions inked on the calendar during May and the first week of June have come to an end. The calendar is relatively clear for the next twelve weeks.

That's just as well. By this time of year, most people can feel for a young man I know who was urged to attend one of the banquets with his family. The thought of the good food which would be served tempted him. "But," he wondered, "how long will the meeting part last?"

His mother didn't know. There would be the usual recognition awards and a speech...

"A speech!" he groaned. "I'd rather have a sandwich at home. I don't like to be bored."

Neither do I. And if I had to think about all the hours I've spent being bored at meetings and banquets I would go out of my mind.

Lest after-dinner speakers take offense, let me add that while I have been among the bored, I'm sure I have also been the borer now and then. We can't all be that rare and gifted person who lifts hopes and dreams and makes imaginations soar with after-dinner speech.

Being bored is no fun, but being the speaker is often no great shakes either. For one thing, unless you are the President of the United States, it can be lonely work. No one talks to you before the speech. In fact, they cluster at the far side of the room, avoiding so much as a glance in your direction if they can. Even acquaintances stand at a distance, eyeing you the way they might a stranger with cholera or some other dread disease.

Only program chairmen talk to you. That is because they have to. No one else will sit at the head table--set for ten--in order to pass the salt.

One program chairman was very frank about all this. She asked me to give a book review for her club which was to meet in two weeks.

I demurred. I haven't read a good book lately, I said, and two weeks was hardly time enough to find a book, read it, and prepare a good review.

"That's all-right," she said. "It doesn't matter if its good or not. Just talk away for 30 minutes. No one will be listening to you anyway."

HEAD TABLE 47

14. The Wave

Someone has suggested that I discuss the art and etiquette of the wave as practiced in the greater Fremont area. A discourse on the various styles of waves in current use as well as pointers on when to wave and when not to wave will benefit newcomers in the community who, through ignorance of local customs, might otherwise wave at the wrong people, or, what is worse, not wave at all.

At the present time, there are four types of waves in general use. Each wave can be embellished at any time according to the mood of the waver and/or his relationship with the person on the receiving end of the wave—better known as the wavee. As a general rule, wavers select one type of wave from among those available, and stick to that one. However, they have no obligation to do so.

Here are the four types of waves: 1. The Basic Handlift. Hand is raised at face level, palm out, fingers straight. Smile is optional. It is a good all-around wave that permits refinements like spread fingers or the back and forth hand cock.

2. The Arm Raise. Arm is extended full length above the head, hand cocks, as in a variation of the basic hand lift, or flutters rapidly. Rarely if ever is it employed without an accompanying smile. Very popular among hale-fellow-well-met types. Occasionally used by persons who usually basic handlift. The waver should know the wavee

by name when using the arm raise wave since conversation often follows. This is the only wave style which requires a name-calling relationship.

3. The Finger Waggle. A personal preference wave, closely related in form to the basic handlift, and useful for all occasions. With or without a smile. The open and shut wave with fingers stiff rather than waggling is considered a variation of this wave rather than a type of its own.

Italians use the open and shut wave with the back of the hand rather than the fingers toward the wavee. I've always wanted to try that wave here, just as I've always wanted to say "Caio!" instead of "Hi!" But I hesitate to do so for fear it would embarrass the family.

4. The Finger Lift. Forefinger lifted straight up while the rest of the hand rests on the steering wheel. Limited, for obvious reasons, to use when the waver is driving a vehicle. Most apt to be accompanied by a tight-lipped grimace; rarely, if ever, seen with a smile.

While this wave is most usually seen at the end of a hard day, it is also in common use among those who habitually drive down a busy street during rush hour. Generally regarded as no less friendly than the hand lift or the finger waggle, wavees should understand this wave is not intended as a snub, but rather expresses the low energy level of the waver.

A slight difference in how one tilts the head and how broadly one smiles gives a considerable range of expression in rendering all four styles of wave. The accomplished waver is able to convey not only something of his or her own personality, but also the mood of the moment and the waver's relationship to the wavee.

As the reader will have noted, the wave type one uses is entirely up to the discretion of the waver. However, occasions for waving are more rigidly proscribed. Rules governing the use of the wave follow.

Nine out of ten of all wavers wave from a motor vehicle. On a run downtown for milk and a newspaper, a waver will normally wave at three pedestrians, two school crossing guards--or two crossing guards four times--one and a half city workers, one police patrol car, and eight other vehicles. These are my figures and will not stand up under audit. All pedestrians, guards, and city workers, and six of the vehicles will wave back.

Actually, the vehicles themselves don't wave, the people in them do. But the windshields on most cars prevent one from making a positive identification of the occupants until it is too late to get off a decent wave, so the well-versed waver waves at the cars he or she knows.

Since several people have vehicles of the same color and make, the waver needs to wave at all of them in order to not slight the one. This may explain why the finger lift is becoming more popular.

Rule #1 then, is wave at all vehicles which have any resemblance to the vehicles of people you know.

Rule #2. Wave only at city workers that you know personally. They have a lot of broken branches and brush from the last ice storm to grind into wood chips these days and can't be waving at every Tom, Dick, and Mary who drives by.

Rule #3. Wave at bicyclists you know, but don't expect them to wave back. If they do wave back, prepare for sudden stops since not everybody in Fremont—or anywhere else—can ride one-handed.

Rule #4. Wave at walkers but don't expect them to wave back either. They may be thinking of something else, they may be too tired from walking, or from waving at the previous five hundred cars that have gone by, or they may not be able to see through your windshield and know that you have waved at them. Many walkers choose to preserve their waving energy until they are sure.

Rule #5. Wave at joggers. You never know what to expect from them and I can't tell you.

Rule #6. Wave at school crossing guards each time you pass them, whether you know them or not. They will soon recognize you car and it is nice to let them know you appreciate the care they give our children. Any basic wave will do.

However, if you forget your purse and have to go back, and then remember your glasses and have to go back, it is permissable on the fifth time you pass the same crossing guard to offer a sheepish grin instead.

Rule #7. Wave at all local police patrol cars. It may be Jim or LeRoy. Or perhaps Dougy who was in my Cub Scout den just last year. Or so it seems.

In addition to these five basic rules for when to wave, there are occasions for optional waves which may be tossed off at the discretion of the waver.

For instance, I always wave at bearded men on the off chance that underneath that growth there is someone I know. A friend of mine waves at

THE WAVE 53

truck drivers because she thinks they must be lonely. A number of people, I notice, now wave at Consumer's Power vehicles out of gratitude since the big ice storm. And several teenagers wave at absolutely everybody, just in case.

Passengers in vehicles, by the way, are not required to wave at all. They may return a wave but they aren't required to do so by the rules.

As captain of the ship, so to speak, the driver has the responsibility of making all decisions, including who to wave at. If the passenger should wave, the driver is distracted from his business at hand by trying to see who was waved at, often at great risk to all concerned.

The driver may even ask "who was that?" This forces the passenger to either make up a name, or admit he doesn't know—something which should be avoided if possible.

I personally rarely wave when I am a passenger. But this may be because my hands are clasped in an attitude of prayer—depending upon who's driving, of course.

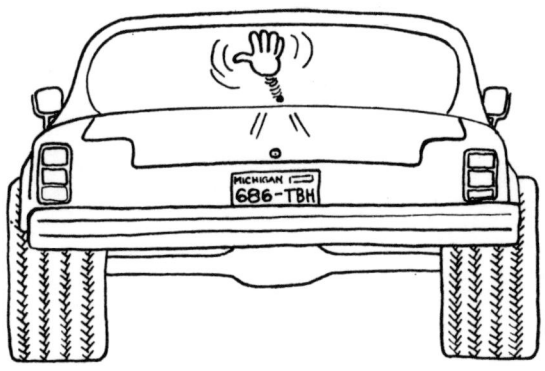

15. Do They Run in the Family?

Last year about this time I went downtown on a rainy day. Water was leaking through the canopy of the Old State Drive-in Bank, the Valueland grocery store had pails set about on the floor to catch drips from the roof, and there were even water problems at the Post Office.

We have a leak too, at the place where our family room joins the kitchen. Some day I expect the family room to separate from the rest of the house and slide down the back hill; that much water comes in on a rainy day.

We have had the roof fixed a dozen times by different roofers, both amateur and professional. They have caulked it, tarred it, copper flashed it, asbestos roofed it. It still leaks.

On ordinary rainy days, I put the roaster on the floor to catch the water. When we are expecting guests, I use a plastic pail and my best towel from the upstairs bathroom. The pail doesn't catch the water as well as the roaster does, because the leak is long and narrow. But with the best towel under the leak, it looks better.

I know a family on the south side of town who have a leak in their living room. They had the roof fixed seven times before folding screens became fashionable. Now they have a folding screen in front of their leak and they just don't bother about the roof. I've never thought to look behind the screen to see whether they use a roaster or a pail.

The couple around the corner have a leak in their upstairs bedroom. They are still young and they think they are going to be able to fix it before they pull off the rest of the wallpaper and redecorate the room. Ha!

I once met a landscape painter who said frankly that he sold his paintings to cover damp spots on walls. I think my father may have bought one of his paintings. He has had a leak in his dining room for fifty years. Do you suppose leaks run in the family? Last week a roofer was boiling tar in my father's yard for still another attempt to repair that leak. Hope springs eternal in the human breast.

Our own leak, placed as it is in the doorway between two rooms, can't be hidden by a folding screen or a landscape painting. A friend suggested we play sparkling music, shine colored spotlights on the water, and charge admission to the show.

I don't intend to go that far, but I do think I'll buy a better looking roaster this spring.

16. Shopping Blues

The holiday season has a way of forcing itself upon you whether you want to notice it or not. Christmas carols ring out in downtown Fremont, decorations festoon the street, Christmas lights are lit. A certain frantic expression creeps into the eyes of the shoppers, and the news that 100,000 people did their Christmas shopping at Woodland Mall in Grand Rapids on Saturday makes you glad that you were here, not there.

Some years ago one of our sons joined the Christmas shopping multitudes for the first time in his young life with a rather memorable and, perhaps, typical if temporary flush of generosity.

He was eight at the time, and in his mitten was clutching ten dollars he'd gotten for his birthday. He set forth for the Ben Franklin store and was gone from home long enough for us to grow anxious about him.

Just as we were about to send a big brother out to look for him, he burst through the door, snow-covered, tear-stained, and racked by great heart-rending sobs.

Moments passed before he could even speak. Was he sick? we asked. Had he been hit by a car? Beaten? Robbed? There didn't seem to be blood on him anywhere. Had he been snubbed by Santa Claus?

"No-o-o!" he wailed in answer to each question. He sat down in his little rocking chair and rocked back and forth in agony, crying at the top of his lungs.

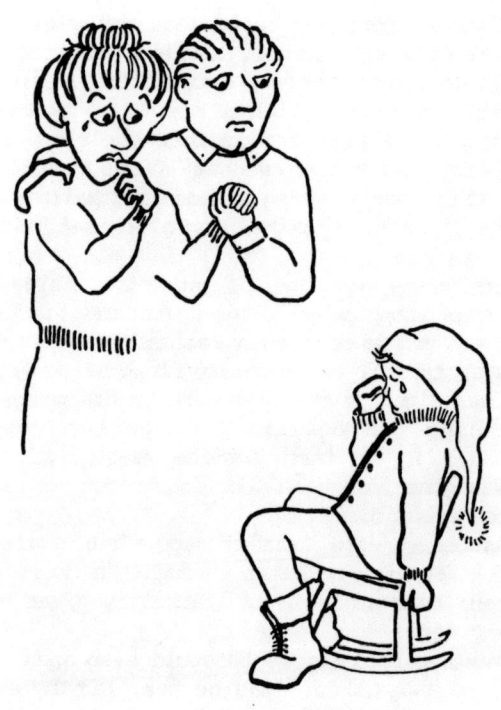

What then? we asked, wiping his tears. What dreadful thing had happened on his first Christmas shopping trip downtown.

The sobs subsided at last and he got the story out. He'd gone to the Ben Franklin store and looked at everything. He made his choice of gifts, something for each one in the family, and had taken them to the checkout counter.

"Ah, then," someone put in helpfully—the whole family had gathered around to help him through this terrible experience, whatever it was—"you didn't have enough money to pay for everything."

"No-o-o, that wasn't it," he said. And he began to cry again. "I had enough money. I got 26 cents back."

"Then what?"

"My ten dollars is all gone," he said. "All the way home all I could think about was the ten dollars I didn't have anymore. I thought I'd have some left to buy something for me, but it's all gone."

"Did you cry like that all the way home?" a big brother wanted to know.

"I didn't cry, but I whimpered a lot," he said.

Which is probably what a lot of us feel like doing when we've finished up our Christmas shopping for another year.

17. Sorry I asked

A series of articles in the "Christian Science Monitor" recently discussed the big cost and big waste of big government in the United States. The U.S. Treasury, according to the Monitor, spends more than a billion dollars a day. A Billion, with a b.

Among other wasteful expenditures, there are more than 70 advisory commissions in the field of energy alone; 2,000 public information people on salary and expense accounts; 743 sub-cabinet level bureaucrats driven to and from work in Washington in government owned cars--a small fringe benefit which is supposed to be against the law--and so many departments and bureaus in existence they can't even identify themselves.

Hundreds, if not thousands, of these people are retiring every day on full pension, to make room for a flood of others who are going on the government payroll.

When you stop to think about it, a billion dollars a day just hardly seems enough to support all that.

With this problem on my mind, I endeavored to conduct a little survey at a party the other evening to discover how a few local couples economize. I hoped their ideas might help some of the rest of us cut down on our spending so we could better afford to send more tax dollars to the needy government.

We do want to keep those government employees

and elected officials enjoying life in the manner to which they've become accustomed, don't we?

The first man I interviewed stated that he never bought a suit at full price. His wife cast about in her mind for ways she economized and came up with nothing. But she pointed out that he did too buy a suit at full price when he went to his son's wedding ten years before.

He said he chose to forget that suit because it was black. Besides that, it got completely covered with hair from the bride's mother's pet collie.

She said it wasn't her fault that lapels got wider the very next year, and the marriage didn't work out anyway.

On that rather unexpected note, I decided to slip away and approach someone else with the same question.

"I read the ads and shop in all the grocery stores for the best bargain," the next woman said.

"Burning up all the money she saves in the gas tank driving from store to store," her husband put in with a kindly chuckle. At least I thought his chuckle was kindly.

"Well, I don't notice you coming up with any way to economize," his wife said rather testily.

"I'm always economizing," he claimed. "You get my whole paycheck every week and I'm left to get by on my wits. I know how to manage without money in a thousand different ways."

"Name one," she said between clenched teeth.

Without waiting for his reply, I left them to their discussion and crossed the room to a larger and, I hoped, friendlier group of women without men.

"I never buy necessities," one member of the group advised. I buy luxuries only. It is incovenient when you go to make sandwiches, but, as Marie Antoinette said, you can always eat cake--or something like that."

"My wife does all the economizing in our family," volunteered a stray husband who had just walked up to the group. "I give her $25 a week to feed our family of six and let her do anything she wants with whatever money she has left over." He gave me a generous smile.

His wife, the cadaverous looking woman hovering over the snack table, was stuffing her pockets with cheese and did not appear to hear.

"I make out a budget and stick to it," another woman said. "The only way to go."

"Budget? Ha!" her husband shouted from his position near the punch bowl some twenty feet away. "She doesn't know the meaning of the word."

His comment led to heated words between them and the atmosphere was still tense when I left the gathering a quarter of an hour later.

As you have by now surmised, my little survey met with something less than total success. If I wish to pursue this line of questioning, I will probably need to divide my subjects according to gender and sequester them in separate rooms.

The National Science Institute awards grants for research on various subjects. For a quarter of a million I could learn some interesting things about economizing.

18. Ah, Those Sentimental Tears!

One of my mother's friends from years ago was a real card. She used to embarrass me whenever she saw me in a large group by shouting out, "Nancy, do you still cry a lot?"

Then she'd laugh and tell about the time she was walking past our house on her way downtown and saw me sitting on the front steps with my doll, crying my eyes out. "Nancy, are you having a wonderful time?" she asked.

"Yes," I sobbed.

Among other tear-drenched episodes, I recall the times my sister and I used to sit at the piano and sing a World War I ballad called, "Just Break the News to Mother."

The verse told about a young man lying on the battlefield, fatally wounded. As he lay there dying--the illustration of the dying boy on the front cover of the sheet music was hand-tinted in three pastel colors which we thought touchingly old-fashioned--he said, or sang, as the case may be, "Just break the news to mother. She knows how much I love her. Tell her I'll not be coming home..."

Neither one of us can remember the last line of the chorus --we were never able to finished it for our tears.

This tendency for sentimental tears must run in the family. Our daugher, who represents the second generation to love "Gone With The Wind", has read the book five times and seen the movie ten times. She is just like Pavlov's dog that salivates when it hears the bell. Her eyes run when she sees the title of the book or even any part of it.

We both enjoy a good cry over sad books, movies, and other stirring events. When the Fremont high school football team made their first touchdown last fall after two no-score seasons, it was probably the first time in all football history that the team manager cried when the team scored. I know she cried because the team manager was our daughter. I was in the stands and I cried too.

Most sentimental weepers cry at weddings. I happen to be immune to tears on that one occasion, but when you consider reports that 75 out of every 100 marriages these days are expected to end in divorce, perhaps I should take up crying then too.

Country music seems to jerk more tears than any other kind. It reminds me of that World War I ballad I cried to in my youth, and I often have a country music station tuned in on the car radio. So if you should see me driving down Main Street some day crying my eyes out, don't worry. I'm probably listening to some sad and sentimental country song, and having a wonderful time.

19. Home for the Holidays

We had three laundries come home from school for Thanksgiving this year. Our two sons brought theirs, of course, and one of them brought the laundry of a friend who lived too far away to go home. The friend himself didn't come. He had a previous invitation.

I knew from my own student days that every time I went home, it was love me, do my laundry. What I didn't remember was how much laundry one student can accumulate between holidays.

No reasonably bright mother would plan to have wash day coincide with every single holiday that comes along, but that is the way it works when the kids go away to school.

She has to sort laundry and stuff the turkey; blanch almonds and bleach the sheets; peel potatoes and pair socks. She is called on to run fifteen to twenty loads of wash while she whips up a feast for thirty people.

Grocery stores must stock extra bleach for the holiday trade. Surely our sons can't be the only ones who toss clothes of all colors into the same wash load in the campus coin-op machines. After a few weeks of such undiscriminating treatment, everything--jeans, underwear, shirts, sheets, socks--everything, blends into the same medium gray.

Friends tell me the situation gets worse with time. When students marry they still bring their laundry home. Not only their own laundry, but

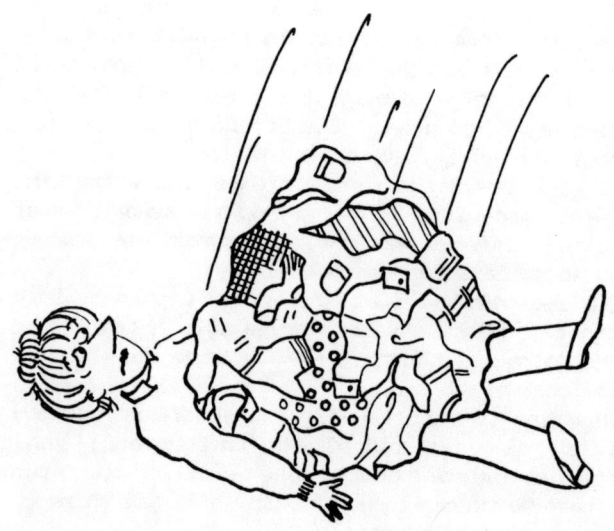

their spouse's, and also every single sheet they received as a wedding gift. There seems to be an unwritten law that young married students never come home for a visit till all their sheets are dirty.

In a well ordered household—alas, ours will never be one—the visiting students do their own laundry. It is possible to tolerate this, I'm told, if the holiday is a short one. But if it goes beyond two days, the pile of laundry begins to haunt the hapless mother; a mute, medium-gray reminder that there is work to be done. And she will be the one who has to do it. She knows her visitors' penchant for putting things off, and dreads the moment—usually midnight before their dawn departure to resume their studies—when they'll suddenly realize they've not done the laundry yet, and cry for help.

Time solves such problems, however. Students are not students forever. Before we know it, it will be their turn to wash the Thanksgiving laundry themselves.

20. Self Improvement

One reason you haven't heard from me just lately is that I've been improving myself. This self-improvement program has been going on for a long time, but the situation came to a head a few months ago when I realized my fortieth high school class reunion was coming up. If I didn't tell you how many years it's been since I graduated from high school, someone else would.

Those forty years, I suddenly realized, have rocketed past. The next forty will probably go even faster. If I'm ever going to make something of myself, I'd better do it now.

Over the years my personal pursuit of self-improvement has met with small success. Before I reached my teens I was sending for 10 cent samples of freckle remover and taking tap dancing with assorted friends from Virginia Grant in the upstairs bedroom of our house. I still have the freckles, though they don't show much anymore among the wrinkles, and no one has asked me to tap dance, ever.

My mother exposed me to all sorts of lessons for the improvement of mind, body, and soul. It was she who took me aside on the eve of my wedding to offer last minute advice: "Read TIME," she said with a note of despair in her voice. "Then at least you'll have something to talk about. I've done all I can."

It was evident she regarded me as an unfinished product. One of her less successful efforts, you might say. I've been trying to complete the job on her behalf ever since.

To that end I have taken courses in millinery, efficient housekeeping, graphology, child psychology, tennis, ballet, piano, Spanish, mind control, group encounter, abstraction in art and nature, needlepoint...the list goes on and on. You name a subject and I have probably taken a course in it.

Did I tell you all this before? Well, never mind. I've signed up for a memory course this fall.

Unfortunately, as indicated earlier, I've not met with unqualified success. Millinery, for instance, was completed just before hats vanished from the fashion scene. One has only to drop in on me without warning on any given day to realize that efficient housekeeping was a total loss.

And there were several years there when I wouldn't have given a plugged nickel for all the hours spent in child psychology. Fortunately, in spite of my efforts, the children turned out well.

I finally failed in Spanish on a busy downtown street in Granada in Spain. We were lost in the thick of the downtown traffic. "There's a policeman across the street," Hartman, my travelling companion, suddenly announced. He seized the opportunity as a drowning man clutches at a rope. "Get out!" he said. "Ask him directions."

"Me?" I quavered. The only foreign phrase I could think of on the spot was "C'est la vie" and that was French, I thought.

"You!" he said. Hartman can be very commanding at times. "Hurry up! The light's changing. You've been studying Spanish for the last three years. Ask him the way to the Alhambra."

I could see myself marooned for days in downtown Granada, casting about in my now blank mind for the proper Spanish words to connect me once more with my husband who was on the point of disappearing down the boulevard in his little rented car.

"Out! Out!" he said, confident that the words would come to me once I found myself face to face with the Spanish police. "I'll drive around the block and meet you here."

Horns began to blow behind us. I froze with my hand on the door of the car. I prayed for one Spanish phrase to surface in my mind and unlock the mental block. I would have been grateful for "Buenos Días" or even "Sí señor," but nothing came. I would still be there but for the kind intervention of fate. Hartman was forced to move on with the traffic with me still in the car, and at the next corner an arrow with the word "Alhambra" pointed the way.

I also flunked Basket Weaving 101 at Michigan State--a sorry episode which has given Hartman, who managed to get through State without flunking anything, a great deal of pleasure.

Also in my catalog of failures is the knee injury that I sustained a year ago in tennis class. It still hurts. However, I confess with some pride that it was an athletic injury. Previously my most athletic moments occurred when I walked from the typewriter to the kitchen sink.

But such minor failures haven't daunted me. I

still sign up for lessons left and right. You might compare it to the game of golf--class meets Wednesday afternoons--in which each time you step up to the tee you think this is the time you'll par the hole. Or at least make it under ten.

It hasn't happened yet to me, but I hope to get this game of life down pat soon. The high school class reunion that's coming up has made me realize how fast time flies.

21. Diet Everyone?

Everyone seems to go on a diet in January. If they aren't on a diet because of low blood sugar, high blood pressure, diabetes, anorexia, or some other human affliction, they are on a diet to lose weight.

Diets are on my mind because I'm on one this January too. It is nothing new. I go on a diet every morning of my life before I get out of bed. "Today," I tell myself as I snuggle under the covers for one last ten-minute snooze, "you are going to eat only at mealtimes, and not much then. In four weeks you'll lose eleven pounds and you can reward yourself with anything you want to eat until you gain one of them back."

I have yet to earn such a reward. I stay on my diet until mid-morning when I start rummaging about the kitchen, looking for something to eat. Anything, even a stale cracker, will do, although I prefer a dozen or two cookies.

The diet I'm not following this time is called the Pritikin Diet chosen because I like vegetables and because I know someone who lost seventeen pounds by following that diet for one month. Chronic dieters love a success story.

The particulars of the Pritikin Diet can be found in a paperback book in the library. There are also seventeen other reducing diets on the library shelves, and a dozen paperbacks on various diets for sale downtown. These diet titles—I'm under the impression they call books 'titles' in the book world--include the murdered Dr. Tarnhower's "Scarsdale Diet," the effervescent Richard Simmons' "Never Say Diet," the "Beverly Hills Diet" which isn't supposed to be good for you, and a "Thin Book By A Formerly Fat Psychiatrist" diet. I'm going to try that one next.

If one happens to be a physician or a celebrity, writing a best-selling diet book must be a cinch. First, there is the encouraging chapter designed to whip up enthusiasm and assure us fat folk that the author knows how tough it is to lose weight.

Chapter two promises the moon. If you follow the recommended regime, whatever it is, you'll feel better, look terrific, hold winning cards at bridge, and never go hungry.

Next comes the list of recommended foods, the foods to be avoided, sample menus, and then recipes. After writing a final inspirational chapter which includes a review of the marvelous things that happen to fat people after they become thin, all the author has to do is stay in the limelight. The book will make him or her a mint.

Perhaps Dr. Tarnhower, who was shot by his jealous mistress did go a bit far to stay in the limelight, but his dramatic demise helped to keep the Scarsdale Diet book on the best-seller list for weeks.

The foods recommended for the Pritikin Diet are fresh fruits, whole grains, infinitessimal amounts of chicken and fish, and bushels of chopped vegetables. All those vegetables must be not only chopped but chewed. I didn't know, when I chose the Pritikin diet from the lot on the book shelves, just how much time it takes out of one's life to be a vegetarian. I should have known from observing both the lion and the cow.

The carnivorous lion can be found loafing under the banyan tree three days out of four. On the fourth day, if the lion is lucky, he snags a passing antelope, shares the kill with other members of his pride, and goes back to rest, satisfied for several days.

The herbivorous cow, on the other hand, must be at it constantly. The cow has teeth especially designed for its diet, as well as four stomachs. But even though equipped with such splendid accessories, it must devote nine-tenths of its life to eating. I'm afraid I look like I have several stomachs too, which is why I go on a diet every day.

We omnivorous humans can eat almost anything except, perhaps, the diet books themselves. We determine our diets by circumstance--some of us are, tragically, truly hungry--by culture, or by choice.

In the United States, most of us can determine our diets by choice. And like the lion, we grab our protein on the run, using most of the time in our lives to pursue something else. Few of us are as willing as the cow to devote so much time to champing and chewing.

Which is why I'm doomed to keep those eleven extra pounds forevermore.

22. On an Empty Nest

"One man in his time plays many parts," Shakespeare wrote, "his acts being seven ages. At first the infant...then the whining schoolboy...And then the lover, sighing like a furnace... Then a soldier...seeking the bubble reputation..." and so on through all seven ages. It is a famous passage, and true, as are so many passages that Shakespeare wrote.

Just now I am coming on stage for what Shakespeare would call Act or Age Five. We know it as the phase of the empty nest. Like everyone else entering into a new experience, I wonder how I'll do.

As luck would have it, I have been surrounded by competent people most of my life. Our children were able to drive better than I could before they reached the age of ten--or so they said. They could open jars, kill hornets, charge batteries without batting an eye, while the thing I did best when faced with an emergency was take a nap until someone in the family came home. I had never even backed up a trailer until this summer, and only did it then because there was no one else within five miles who could be trusted with the job.

My seeming incompetence puts an awful responsibility on my legal housemate, Hartman, who, due to the presence of the children for the last twenty-five years, has never become fully aware of how inept I really am. The empty nest phase could turn out to be as difficult for him as it is supposed to be for me.

Dozens of people we know have already gone through it, however, so I know it can be done.

As a matter of fact, I have been preparing myself for the new phase for months. I have backed up the trailer in the driveway two dozen times in a row, developed fity-two new skills, resurrected twelve old ones, taken on two new hobbies, laid in a supply of small pots and pans, learned to do my own dishes, and practiced answering the telephone all by myself. None of the phone calls are for me yet, but they will be as soon as word gets around that the line is not busy.

ON AN EMPTY NEST

Except for the very depressing article that I read on "When the Last Child Leaves Home," which cited divorce as the only answer, I thought I was ready to make it into Age Five fairly well.

But our daughter, the bird who has just flown the nest, was not certain. Before she left for collge, we chanced to meet in front of the drugstore downtown. She examined me for flaws then picked a piece of hay out of my hair. "Mother," she said, "besides that, you have crumbs in your cowl.

"Who is going to do this for you when I´m gone?" she went on with a worried sigh.

The question lingered in my mind like the contents of that depressing article for a day or two. But then at the checkout counter of the local Safeway grocery store, I was reassured.

"Mrs. Johnson," one of the bag boys said, "you have something on your eyebrow."

I stepped back in alarm. Something alive? Would it bite? Did it look poisonous?

"Just a little feather or something," he said reassuringly.

I brushed it off myself. It was a bit of shell from the shrimp I´d been shelling earlier in the day.

I must write my daugher to tell her not to worry; as long as I´m among friends, I´ll get along just fine.

23. Off to the Rally

Recently Hartman and I were in Asheville, North Carolina, on business and met Judy Anthrop of Holland, Michigan. Judy owns Janthrop Antiques in West Olive. We had met Judy before in Milwaukee, Kansas City, Grand Rapids, and, for all I know, Pittsburgh. She is a member of an American subculture, the weavers, with whom we do business in our handweaving loom factory in Fremont.

Cities like Milwaukee and the rest are either irregular yellow shapes or small circles with or without black dots in the center. Place names are important to me right now for reasons which will become clear presently.

Judy introduced us to Barbara McFall. People names are not so important for our purposes here, except to the people who own them, without which they would not know who they are.

Barbara is navigator for Judy in the road rally race called the Saugatuck Madness which takes place every year toward the end of October in Saugatuck, Michigan. Saugatuck. A small circle without a dot. On a blue road.

When I found out what Barb does in October, my admiration for her knew no bounds. I admire her not only for navigating in the Saugatuck Madness, but for entering the race more than once on a volunteer basis, for finishing it without bursting into tears, and for being on speaking terms with the driver when it is all over.

In case you don't know any more about road rallies than I did before Judy told me, I pass on these facts: The course is laid out by a Rally Master. The object of the race is to complete the course with the same mileage as the Rally Master in as short a time as possible, not to exceed six hours. Failing that, you must complete the course anyway, no matter how long it takes, or you will be ashamed of yourself.

Time, not speed, is the important consideration. Entrants must check in at specified check-points, fulfill certain requirements of the course, and at every intersection make `major-minor´ and `hare-hound´ decisions.

My intense admiration for navigator Barb, whose car has more than once `showed´ at the Saugatuck Madness, is based on personal experience. At least once during every road trip such as the weaving business trips I've mentioned above, I've found myself cast in the role of navigator for a road rally race of our own. I don't qualify for the position because I can't turn the right way out of a motel room door. But lack of qualification is no excuse.

Certain conditions prevail at these Johnson rallies: the weather is always hot and humid; the air-conditioning is always out of order in the vehicle; we are driving through a city in the rush hour traffic; we are tired; and we have no time to spare.

Our most recent event, which we called the `Louavull Luck-aout,´ took place in Kentucky as we were returning from the Asheville weavers´ conference where we met Judy again. All the conditions mentioned before prevailed. I was called to the starting point by a frantic cry from the driver, Hartman. "Detour!" he cried. "What did that sign say?"

My heart clutched and my eyes blurred as I snatched up the map which has become frayed, wrinkled, and tear-stained from the stresses of previous rallies.

"I didn't see it," I yelled over the roar of wind and traffic. Right away, I gave offense. One could not even shout "I love you" under those circumstances without making the driver mad.

"Highway 60" he shouted. "It said 60. Left, right, or straight ahead?" This is known as a hare-hound decision in road rally circles. Barb McFall would probably know what to do, but I choked up and stared at the map in frantic desperation. Five lanes of traffic swarmed by us on either side.

"Fort Knox," Hartman said. "Do we want 60 toward Fort Knox?"

"There is no such thing as Fort Knox," I said.

"You've got the map. It's on the map."

"It is not on the map," I said.

Such conversations conducted at top voice on a hot day on a busy freeway around Louisville are not fruitful.

I made a major-minor decision. "Get off the highway," I hollered. "Take 60, next right."

Wrong. We did not want Fort Knox, which suddenly appeared on the map in red letters.

Forty-two traffic lights later, all of them red, we were back on the freeway hurtling toward the other end of Highway 60 which finally appeared disguised as the road to Hamburg, a small circle between two tear drops on a blue road. The situation between the rally driver, Hartman, and the rally navigator, me, remained tense for several hours.

We have a 1922 Automobile Bluebook such as might be found in the Janthrop Antiques shop. Route 638 from Shelby to Grand Rapids reads in part:

Miles
- 19.9 Four corners; picnic grove on left; left.
- 23.9 Four corners; right.
- 30.8 End of road; left
- 31.5 Fremont. Main & Division Sts at Bank Ahead (east) on Main St.
- 31.7 Four corners; beyond school; right.

I should have been travelling in 1922; I could follow directions like that.

24. The Absent Mind

Recently a ten-year old Ypsilanti boy was the object of an all night search after his frantic mother reported him missing. He turned up at the breakfast table the next morning. He'd slept all night at one of the neighbor's. His mother had said he could.

Poor woman. She has a mind like mine; it leaks like a sieve. Important details, like the whereabouts of your children, the last known locations of your eyeglasses, and the name of the item you went to the store for run right out of the head, leaving it clogged with useless information like the altitude of Durango, Colorado—6,000 feet.

I can't remember where I left the car in the mall parking lot, or, in some instances, what car I was driving when I parked it, but I sure can tell you how old Rex Stout was when he wrote the first Nero Wolfe mystery—48.

I have never, ever, stepped out of a motel room and turned the right way, but just ask me how to get from Uxmal to Xlapac in the Yucatan peninsula in Mexico. I can tell you that in a minute. The trouble is, I never need to go there.

I once dialed the dry cleaners and asked them to pick up the cleaning. I then hung up the phone, picked it up again, dialed the dry cleaners and asked them to pick up the cleaning. There was a long silence on the other end of the line the second time I called. They were probably wondering down there at the cleaners whether or not to call the police.

The announcement on TV: "Parents, do you know where your children are?" makes me nervous. A lot of the time, I don't even know where I am.

Our children couldn't even get their teeth straightened until they were old enough to tell me how to get to Grand Rapids. I have yet to take the right exit off I-96. Or the right turn off East Maple, for that matter. I'm the only person I know who can get lost in Fremont.

Names are another problem. The very thought of making an introduction drains my mind completely. Fortunately for my ego, I'm not the only one. I'm not even the only one who gets mixed up on faces. Half the people I meet downtown call me Marj. Whoever she is.

I don't bother to correct them, even when the conversation gets personal. I fake it. I don't want it to be my fault if Marj seems unfriendly.

I wonder if she enjoyed those folks I asked over for supper last night.

25. Hidden Message

The gifts we give convey hidden messages, according to a psychoanalytic psychotherapist named Kogan who was quoted in an article about gifts in "Glamour Magazine." Kogan also talked about the meaning of gifts as a guest on the Today Show. Pop psychology is everywhere.

According to Kogan, a gift not only tells us what the giver of a gift thinks of us, but also reveals the current state of relationship between the giver and the receiver. Gift giving, he claims, is a form of communication.

The right gift says, "I like you just the way you are." It takes a lot of caring to give the right gift. You must not only know the person who is to receive the gift well enough to know what he likes, you must be able to find what he likes, and having found it, you must be able to afford it.

On the other hand, the wrong gift says, "I wish you were different." Subconsciously, perhaps, the giver may wish the receiver were a Pac-Man freak instead of a reader of romantic novels. Or a mechanical wizzard instead of a bird watcher. He then gives the bird watcher a set of tools and the reader of romantic novels a roll of quarters with which to play the game of Pac-Man. So says Kogan.

His idea that there is a hidden message in gifts not only adds another dimension to the art of gift giving, it could affect the way one receives a gift--an art in itself--as well.

Take the case of the ugly bedroom slippers. Several years ago, Hartman, the man I live with,— a phrase which appears frequently in Glamour Magazine articles— gave me a pair of ugly bedroom slippers for Christmas.

In our more than three decades of living together, he has earned super ratings in the art of gift giving. But on this particular Christmas, the slippers he gave me looked like they might have been given to an ancient crone with foot trouble who didn't like them either, and who had returned them to the store. The gift puzzled me, but I gave our gift recipient's standard response number 1 and wore them anyway.

We have two standard responses to unlikely gifts at our house. Standard response no. 1 is a hearty "Now THERE is a necktie--or ashtray, or pair of bedroom slippers," or whatever followed by a brave and cheery "Thank you!"

Standard response no. 2 was inspired by a bread and butter letter we received from a young lady a few years back. I quote it in full because it expresses the thought so well:

Dear Mr. and Mrs. Johnson:
　　Thank you for the present. It was something I didn't know I wanted.
　　　　　　　　　　　　Sincerely,

"Ah, thank you!" we say now when standard response no. 2 seems called for. "Something I didn't know I wanted!"

The hidden message notion now adds a third standard response to our repertoire. It can be put to use, no doubt, before the year is out. It has already saved me from shuffling around the house in those ugly bedroom slippers any longer.

I realized, after reading the Glamour Magazine article and listening to Kogan on TV, that there was a message in those slippers I was meant to receive.

"What did Hartman have in mind?" I asked myself the next time I put them on. Had he finally noticed that I have feet of clay?

Whatever the message, I wanted to know what it was, so I told Hartman that I thought those slippers were ugly and I asked him rather testily just what he meant by giving them to me.

He was understandably taken aback. "I don't like them either," he said after a rather lengthy silence. "But I remember now. I'd worked my way up to third in line at the gift wrapping counter and didn't want to lose my place. So I asked a friendly looking fellow who was waiting for his wife if he would go get a pair of slippers in your size. I was going to tell you to exchange them, but you seemed to think they were all right, so I didn't say anything."

That is why standard response no. 3 is needed here. Next time one receives a gift of doubtful taste or usefulness and responses no. 1 and no. 2 don't seem quite appropriate, one can say, "Thank you. What does it mean?"

26. Long Term Storage

A couple of years ago, when faced with the empty nest phase of life one reads about, Hartman, the father of our children, and I moved into a smaller nest. The new nest originally had one closet, three walls of which must have been removed when we added a living room, for we never saw it again.

The shortage of storage space didn't bother us, we were not going to collect anything. After all, we told ourselves, no longer would we accumulate possessions. Henceforth, anything we did not use in the course of twelve months would be sold, given away, or junked. We would never again devote shelf space to chipped tea cups, old golf bags, or bent pieces of aluminum tubing that once had bolts on each end.

All we would require for the rest of our lives, we said, was space for those things we use every day, room at the table for friends, and an extra bed or two for when the children stay over. Without an accumulation of possessions, life would be simple and free.

So much for that line of thought. The chipped tea cups belonged to my favorite great-aunt; one of the kids might want to take up golf some day and would need a golf bag; and perhaps whatever it is that belongs with the aluminum tubing will turn up in one of the cartons we've not yet unpacked. The basement is crammed to the gunwales with the same old boxes of stuff we stored for twenty years in our last house.

Moreover, although our children have left the nest, they have not left the nest empty. They all have possessions of their own which have to be stored. Not only that, but every time they move from one scene to the next—which children often do when they first leave home—there is another collection of items which somehow finds its way back to us.

We are not the only parents of old children so blessed—everyone over 21 who has living parents is an "old child". One friend told me she realized her son had bought a new mattress for his apartment when the old one turned up in her garage. She might not have noticed it among other possessions he stores there, but the mattress fell on her.

Another parent confessed that her daughter's wedding gifts were still stored in her basement. Her daughter was married ten years ago and has since been divorced. Twice.

Parents all over the country are leaving their cars in the driveway, placing floor boards in the attic, and enclosing back porches because their children in transit have brought U-Haul trailers full of stuff home to store.

No parent, however, has been so put-upon as my own. In 1953 Hartman and several of his friends detached an entire truckload of mahogany panels from the main salon of a former Great Lakes cruise ship, the City of Grand Rapids, and stored them in my father's barn.

My father is a man of infinite patience, but he finally got tired of sidling out of his car. He had the panelling removed at his own expense to the basement of his office downtown, where, as far as I know, it reposes still.

Hartman and I are meeting the problem head on at our house. Each time the children cast a shadow on the threshold we urge upon them cartons and bags of their possessions to take away. They plead for time to get their own houses in order. They make excuses. They walk off empty handed whenever they can.

But we stand firm. "Take it away!" we cry. We even deliver from time to time.

Thus, in spite of their resistance, we are making inroads on the colossal collection of clutter that fills our basement. We have to make room in that basement somehow. We still have stuff that belongs to us in my father's barn. We put it there the first three times we moved after we were married back in the '40s. One of these days he's going to come to the end of his infinite patience and tell us to take it away.

27. Yard Sale

Yard and garage sales have been a dime a dozen lately. More than a hundred yard sales were listed in the Newaygo County newspaper want ads in the past two weeks. There must have been almost again that many advertised privately by signs with arrows on them placed at near-by corners. That means a lot of yard sales going on in a county whose total population is under 30,000.

Buying and selling used merchandise without benefit of a middleman must surely be one of the biggest things going among us ordinary folk in the Age of Aquarius. I hope historians, sociologists, and anthropologists take note.

A yard sale or garage sale is a sale of used goods which takes place in either a yard or garage. The only difference between the two is that the garage sale is put on by a pessimist, the yard sale by an optimist. One thinks it is going to rain, the other doesn't.

Such sales are sometimes called moving sales, flea markets, yard give-aways, and garge sales. There are subtle but important distinctions between them. I assume that garge sale began as a sign painter's error for an on-going event south of Fremont. The word 'garge' got the message across and the vendors have been too busy with their customers to change it.

Indeed, it is too late to change it now. Garge has made its way into the local language. People leave notes saying they are shopping at Garge. Or they give directions to the blueberry farm which include "Turn right at Garge."

Yard give-away is also a new modification on the yard sale scene. I liked the ad which said: "All items priceless. Come take what you need and leave a donation if you can."

I did wonder, though, how they hoped to reap one of the prime benefits of a yard sale under such a system, namely, the removal from the premises of excess possessions. Fortunately, before I got the car loaded up with my own donations for that sale, someone suggested that the donations they were hoping for were in the form of cash.

Flea markets are fun. They held one in the parking lot of the First Reformed Church in Fremont on a recent weekend. There were stalls full of the usual clothing, dishes, and household goods, but also baked goods, vegetables, music-- for which there was no charge--, and a car wash.

Before the benefits of the flea market were so widely known, a friend and I went to Ravenna where a flea market has been running every Saturday for years. We loaded a station wagon with used merchandise, along with our two youngest children who were barely out of the strollers we were including in the sale. Innocents we were, in the land of commerce.

Old timers spotted us as we drove in, looked over our goods as we unloaded, and sat back to wait. Late in the day, when our wagon was stuffed beyond capacity with things we'd bought from them, and the two children were crying at the top of their lungs, the old timers came back. We would have paid them to take our merchandise off our hands at that moment. Which they well knew.

A `Moving Sale´ sign suggests selling out to the bare walls. Such sale signs attract the serious yard/garage sale addict especially; the one with a bumper sticker that reads "Caution! This car stops at yard sales". This customer will buy anything except, possibly, two crying kids.

I´m not such an addict, but I did bicycle around the Fremont area yard/garage sale circuit one Saturday. Attending yard sales on a bicycle is a protective technique which works the same way going through a grocery store without a cart does. Which is to say, not very well. You buy everything you think you want anyway and then have the trouble of trying to carry it all.

I learned on my rounds that Saturday that most people who put on yard sales make the sale an annual event. Neighbors are eager to help, and often add their wares to the general display of merchandise to be sold.

Business was slow on the Saturday I took my bicycle tour of the sales, except for one block where a spontaneous outbreak of three yard sales in a row attracted the serious addicts. The slow sales may have been due to the weather.

It was a glorious day, and when a glorious day happens in Michigan, that's all anyone can think about.

28. A Rite of Passage

One May in the early 70´s I was invited to speak to the Juniors and Seniors of Fremont High School at the Junior-Senior Banquet. The Junior-Senior Banquet is one of several traditions which take place each spring to mark the rite of passage known as graduation.

Perhaps it was a sign of the times that the Junior-Senior Banquet that year was not a banquet at all; it was a breakfast. Our young people were in a state of rebellion, it seemed, against all tradition. If classes in Fremont High School had had dinner banquets for fifty years, they would have a breakfast. And breakfast they had.

I agonized for weeks about my speech to those who were taking their first giant step into the larger world since they left home for kindergarten.

The larger world, at the beginning of the 70´s, was in pretty bad shape. We were still deep in the Vietnam War. Cambodia was being set up for its ultimate destruction. The rebels of the 60´s were still in full protest. Plane highjackings were an everyday headline. Violence and threats of violence were so common they did not even make page one.

Parents, in those days, felt as though they were walking through mine fields. They knew too well the pained expression in each others´ eyes and they never asked how the kids were doing. They waited to be told.

Yet as I walked the two blocks from our house to the high school the morning of the banquet breakfast, I could hear the student rock band playing loud and brave—and maybe even well for all I knew about rock. The students heading for the cafeteria with me looked happy and bright with shining faces and shining hair. And shining hope.

Our world, right here, right then, was not all bad.

In tune with the times, however, between the orange juice and the scrambled eggs, Bob Eisner, the high school principal, announced that someone had phoned in to tell him that a bomb had been planted in the school and it was due to go off. Police were searching the lockers; they were sure it was a hoax. But anyone who felt uneasy about the situation was free to leave, he said.

Only one girl picked up her sweater and her purse and hurried out. Everyone else buzzed about it for a moment or two and then settled down to eat their eggs.

The bomb scare was nothing personal, I was sure. I hadn't spoken on the student circuit before so no one could possibly know how bad I was going to be.

And so the banquet-breakfast went on anyway. The shining, hopeful students, the rock band, and the bomb scare are the only things I can remember about the event itself. Whatever I said in my speech, so long in preparation, so agonized about, was forgotten the moment it was over. Even by me.

Yet it is fitting that we observe occasions that surround graduations with words which we hope are appropriate, forgettable as they may be. Attention should be paid to those of us who are ending one phase of our lives, beginning another.

We who have graduated comprise a single long procession through the years; a procession of men and women who have stepped up to receive diplomas for some learning accomplished. It is a procession which reaches back to the time of the ancient Greeks who gave us our first schools and universities. And it is a procession which will continue as long as men and women love learning; as long as mankind survives.

The world was in pretty desperate shape in 1942 when my own high school class graduated in Fremont. Our country was just six months into World War II, and we were ill-prepared for war. The outlook was bleak. Some of the members of the class were already in uniform on commencement day. Some of them never came back.

We can scarcely miss the fact that the world is again--or still--in bad shape today. But our world, right here, right now, is not all bad. Young people are still shining with hope, still graduating. The procession continues along as it has since school began.

I want to add my own forgettable words to the other words the graduates are hearing this May. Attention must be paid to Lyn who received her degree in Nursing last Thursday; to Matthew, Valedictorian of his high school class graduating Tuesday; to Mark and Janet who graduate from Michigan State on Saturday. These young people stand for all the young women and young men who graduate each May.

Those of us who walk before you in the long procession are still learning, as you will be learning for the rest of your lives. We are glad that you are with us. We love you. We support you. We wish you well.

29. A Legendary Tree

Some day, no doubt, the pop psychologists will present for our consideration a study on how people express their personalities by the Christmas trees they put up. People who drape tinsel on their trees, they will say, are outgoing party lovers who enjoy the holidays to the full. Those who trim trees with icicles keep their feelings hidden but are really warm and loving inside. Those who hang their children's homemade ornaments on the tree even after the children are grown are shamelessly sentimental.

People who put up huge trees are open-hearted and expansive, the pop psychologist will probably report, while those who choose small perfectly shaped trees seek order and control of their surroundings.

I can imagine the personality differences which the study would reveal among people who like artificial trees, those who insist on cutting their own natural tree, and those who bring a living tree and its ball of dirt into the house to be planted later when the ground thaws. But we will leave analysis of those particular personality quirks for the pop psychologist.

Right now I have in mind two quite different Christmas trees which may or may not betray the truth about their owners.

The first was a tree put up a quarter of a century ago and it has become legendary in our community. The second was a tree put up only a few years ago at our house and may best be forgotten.

The first tree, erected by a friend named Billie who doesn't need a tree to bespeak her artistic and original nature, stood thirty feet tall in the woods. It had been felled by someone who liked to cut his own tree, and who realized, perhaps too late, that a thirty foot tree would not fit in the trunk of his car. Whatever the reason, he cut the top off the tree and took that, leaving the rest of it in the woods. Billie, who also takes in stray cats and sick houseplants, saw possibilities where no one else would. She arranged to have what was left of the tree--a sturdy trunk with wide spreading branches near its flat top--brought to her house by truck.

Her husband, a man with a stutter who is fondly remembered by all who knew him, wanted nothing to do with whatever Billie had in mind for that tree. It was evening when he saw the truck with the huge tree pull into the yard and he decided to go to bed. It was almost time anyway, and he'd already had a hard day.

But Billie had a strong young son, and together they tackled the herculean task of bringing the tree into the living room. They labored through the night, and when dawn came and Billie's husband emerged from the bedroom, there stood the tree. "I'll b-be d-d-damned," he said. "She d-did get the b-b-blamed thing in the house after all!"

The branches of the tree formed a canopy over the room. Billie festooned them with lights and ornaments. Children came to wonder and to play around its trunk. Friends dropped in to sit beneath the tree and have a cup of tea. Strangers knocked on the door and asked if they could see the sight. There was a Christmas tree, they'd heard, that grew right through the roof. Others said it hung from the ceiling and was never taken down. Stories grew up around that tree which are part of local Christmas lore even today.

One year I thought we might have just such a tree of our own. My long suffering husband, Hartman, rolled his eyes heavenward; he knew which member of the family would go to bed early, and which one would have to get the b-b-blamed thing in the house. He knew also that our strong young sons were too far from home to help.

Nevertheless, I wangled an invitation from the owners of a pine woods who allowed us to choose and cut one of their trees.

The tree I selected was 25 feet tall with a trunk eight inches in diameter, and a dead weight of a quarter ton. The weight was a matter I'd neglected to consider when I was planning the project. Merely getting it out of the woods onto a truck was a job for three men and a horse, as the saying goes. But Hartman and the hapless owner of the pine woods managed to do the job without the horse. They both plannned to be out of town, they told me right then, if I ever came up with an idea like that again.

To make the tree easier to handle, we cut the top and lower branches off before we removed it from the truck. I use the executive "we" here. I'm not good at anything that requires strength, dexterity, and the use of tools. Hartman cut the branches off; I stood by to wring my hands.

Next we fabricated a wooden stand and stood the tree in the garage for a few days to make sure I still wanted to carry on. I did.

Reinforcements were brought in--two more strong men, but no horse. They hauled the tree into the house, and, inflicting only slight damage to the interior of the room, got it to stand upright. It was much too early for me to go to bed while they were doing that, so I went to town to wring my hands instead.

When I returned, I trimmed the tree, looked at it for several hours, and called Hartman who´d gone to the office to avoid whatever was going to happen next. "Perhaps," I said, easing into the subject as tactfully as possible, "the tree is not quite right. Maybe we should look in the woods again just in case there is a better one."

I couldn´t see Hartman´s eyes roll heavenward over the telephone, but I could detect a faint groan on the other end of the line.

In most cases a Christmas tree is like a child. If it is yours, you love it, no matter what. But in this case, I felt no affection for it at all. It had to go. The tree I had in mind was to spread out over the living room, welcoming and sheltering all comers. This tree listed to the north and it looked for all the world like a stalk of broccoli.

I removed the ornaments and lights one by one. "We" cut off more branches to make it easier to remove and then we dragged it outside. Little was said between us as a new tree, purchased at a corner lot, was brought to take its place. At such times in a marriage, silence is the best policy.

Our second tree had the conventional pine-tree shape which reveals, no doubt, that I am not artistic and original but ordinary and old fashioned. I am also blessed with a husband of infinite strength and forbearance, who would never marry anyone like me again.

The lower branches of our second tree were trimmed off in a sort of compromise action so children could play under it. But friends and strangers couldn't sit beneath it unless they happened to be very short. Nevertheless, it was our tree and I loved it.

Our giant stalk of broccoli had a few branches left on the top when it was hauled from the room. Its final trimming had given it the appearance of a palm tree rather than a vegetable. Hartman hung a kerosene lantern on it and set it out by the front door where it became the makings of a legend of our own.

30. Tacky Tacky

A recent newspaper article stated that $50 and $100 bills are enjoying new popularity. To be sure, $50 and $100 bills have always been very popular with me and I'm glad to see that the general public is at last realizing how nice they can be. Of the two, I like $100 bills best. They are so new, clean, and crisp. Not at all like the $1 bills in circulation these days.

We once watched a man in an all-night restaurant poke at a crumpled wad of money with his spaghetti fork in order to find the bills he needed to pay the check. Then he wadded up the rest of his money and put it in a jacket pocket which also contained a few links of greasy chain, some used auto parts, a sandwich and a screwdriver.

Don't ask me how I know what was in his pocket. I'm just guessing. The fact that the restaurant was open all night has nothing to do with the story either. The point is that most of the $1 bills which pass through my hands lately look like they have spent a lot of time in that fellow's pocket. They are torn, dirty, mended with tape, crimped at the corners, and limp as rags.

Not that I want to sound as if I'm too fond of clean money. Racketeers and crooked politicians like clean money so well they send it out of the country to be laundered. A former bank president I once knew carried nothing but spanking clean new bills.

"I never touch dirty, used money," he would say with a flare of his nostril.

At the time, it seemed just a peculiar and interesting facet of his personality. Later we discovered that much of the clean new money he liked to use really belonged to somebody else.

He paid his debt to society and was released from prison some years ago. If still living, he no doubt handles the tattered dirty money in circulation these days with kid gloves, his nostrils in a state of permanent flare.

Such instances force one to conclude that soiled money is somehow more honest. But even so we should not call into question the honesty of the Automatic Teller Machines.

Automatic Teller Machines—known as ATM's—are the new installations in banks. One gets cash from one's account by inserting a plastic card into a slot. In a few years time they will have become so commonplace that it will seem quaint and amusing that I had to explain what they are. ATM's work only with clean new bills.

It is in the customer's best interest to keep ATM's supplied with clean bills. He can, if he must, dirty up the money to make it honest after he takes it from the ATM, but it is not recommended lest there be flaring of nostrils all around.

As with any innovation there are bugs to be ironed out, as indicated by two incidents with an ATM in Wisconsin.

A person who is still at large at this writing, put his or her card into the ATM and hit the jackpot. Some $1,800 came spewing out in response to a twenty-five dollar request. He or she scooped up the money and departed without so much as a thank you ma´am.

The second incident was not even briefly so pleasant for the customer. His card was rejected to due to insufficient funds. He knew this was wrong; he had deposited an $1,800 bonus check just the week before.

After his card had been rejected several times his nostrils not only flared, they smoked. He hauled off and kicked the ATM. Buzzers sounded. Bells rang. Security officers and the police appeared, read him his rights and told him he could tell it to the judge.

In order to forestall such episodes, banks are now hiring full time employees to sort through money to find bills good enough for the pernickety tastes of the ATM. This may be one reason we in the boondocks see so many raunchy looking dollar bills.

In order to protect my reputation, I feel compelled to repeat that I´m not excessively fond of clean money. I just happen to like it better, that´s all. Just as I like one hundred dollar bills better than fifties. Or ones.

But I was moved by the poor condition of the dollar bills to make an inquiry at a local bank. "Why" I asked, "do dollars look so tacky lately?"

Part of a government money-saving ploy, I was told. We the people refuse to use the Susan B. Anthony dollar coins the government thought would be good for us. They look too much like quarters. Even a five-year-old could have told them that. So the life of the paper dollars in circulation must be stretched some other way.

Now when a bank sends a bundle of old, damaged, dirty bills for replacement, the treasury department sends back a different bundle of bills, just as old, damaged, and dirty.

A more honest dollar for a day's work, you might say. But in light of the present day inflation, I don't think you will.

31. A State of Perfect Repair

We have a brick path which runs alongside the garage, under a large maple tree and around to the back of the house. Several years ago one of the bricks began to work itself up. Or rather, the brick was worked up by the root of the maple tree. Last summer it became a stumbling block. One of our visitors stumbled on it while jogging, nearly catapulting through our sliding glass door as a result.

We picked up the brick, set it to one side of the path and left it there for a year. I suppose we thought stepping into a hole might be less painful than catapulting.

A few weeks ago Hartman, who is a grouter—I'll tell you what that is presently—was inspired to do a repair job. He removed several more bricks, brushed away the sand and chopped out the offending root. He then replaced all the bricks and tamped them down.

Such is the work of a grouter. The term was coined, I believe, by Rushworth M. Kidder in a Christian Science Monitor article about people who repair the grout around their bathroom tile themselves instead of 'having a man in' to do the job.

Grouters are a peculiarly American breed, Kidder said. He is a grouter himself but while he was living in England some while ago, he did as the English do and 'had a man in.' The English do not grout; they spend their leisure time gardening or developing personal relationships through conversation. American grouters, who not only repair grout but anything else that needs fixing around the house, have little time for such uplifting pursuits. It is a situation Mr. Kidder rather regrets.

As Hartman, the grouter, and I stood back to admire the finished job on our brick path, it came to our attention that several other bricks were being worked up to the stumbling block stage by the roots of the maple tree.

It is the role of a grouter's spouse to stand by when any projects are undertaken. She must give and take tools, screws, nuts, and bolts upon command, offer words of encouragement, and helpful suggestions.

There is a fine line between helpful suggestions and outright bossiness which even the most experienced grouter's spouse may overstep. This is an opportunity for personal relationships Mr. Kidder may have overlooked.

In this case I encouraged Hartman to renew his efforts on the brick path. More bricks were lifted out of place, more roots revealed and chopped out.

During the chopping process Hartman cracked a bone in his finger when he hit it with a hatchet. If he were a younger man, he said, he would go to a doctor to have the finger fixed. But since he is middle-aged, he would probably only need that finger another 30 years or so and would let it heal by itself. Grouters can often be identified by their scarred and battered hands.

At last the task was finished. The grouter's spouse, as is only fitting, brought him the broom

to sweep away the dirt. She returned the hammer, the hatchet, the chisel, the trowel, and the first aid kit to their proper places. She then praised the finished project with careful moderation. Too much praise borders on irony and is to be avoided at all costs.

Next day it became apparent that Hartman had not only chopped away the roots and broken his finger, but he had cut into the sprinkling system as well. Fortunately, it was a Saturday. He met the new challenge under the brick path with a calm bred by a thousand such challenges over the years.

Dressed in the grouter's uniform—grease-stained trousers and an ancient shirt with battery acid holes in front—he went to the early morning conclave of the grouter's fraternity.

The grouter's fraternity, known locally as the Do-It-Yourselfers, is a national organization of people who make their own repairs. They meet at hardware stores across America at least two or three times every Saturday morning.

It is significant that few of the grouters really know what they want when they go into the hardware store. You can see them any Saturday, talking and gesturing with earnest expressions to the attentive shopkeeper. It is his job to guess what the grouter has in mind. They may also be seen gazing intently at the stock. They'll know what they want when they see it, whatever it is.

Our grouter, Hartman, went to the store to get a whatchamajig to fit inside the newly severed sections of the sprinkling system, and two thingamajigs to hold the whatchamajig in place. The whatchamajig was the size of his forefinger; the one he hadn't broken. Later he went back to get a whatchamajig the size of the broken finger since the first one was too small.

I know several members of the grouter's fraternity very well. Hartman is one. So is my father. So are our sons and our son-in-law. With such a gaggle of grouters in the family, one might think I could go from birth to death with everything in a state of perfect repair. But grouters being grouters, that is a luxury I still have to experience.

I sometimes wonder if it might not be rather pleasant to take the English way out.

32. Radio Alarm

Twenty-one years ago someone gave us a radio alarm clock for Christmas. It told time with a long hand and a short hand that pointed to numbers 1 through 12 arranged clockwise on a round face. The radio turned on without fail every morning including Saturdays and Sundays. Whenever we left the bedroom we turned it off with a knob which said "Off-On". Except on weekends when we turned it off and went back to sleep. The other knobs labelled "set-clock", "set-alarm", and "tune", did just as indicated. The off-on knob also adjusted the volume.

Three or four years ago the set-alarm knob stopped working and we had to re-set the clock if we wanted to get up at a different hour. If we wanted to get up at 7:30 instead of 6:30, for instance, we would set the clock back. The alarm would go off when the clock said 6:30 as usual, but we knew it was really 7:30. If we had to get up earlier than 6:30, we set the clock ahead. No problem, once you master the principle of Daylight Saving Time.

We never got up at the quarter of the hour or the quarter after because that was too complicated. In such cases, we either woke up 45 minutes too early and had a leisurely morning, or 15 minutes too late and hurried a lot.

One day this serviceable piece of equipment spontaneously ended its useful life. We had had a radio alarm clock for so many years we thought it was a basic necessity and at our first opportunity, we purchased a replacement.

The new radio alarm clock has digital numbers, an AM-FM stereo radio, and a number of other features which are explained in a 12-page booklet. It was the simplest model we could find. Most models made coffee, reported the weather, flashed time on the ceiling, and I don't know what all.

It is customary at our house to change the radio alarm clock to the other side of the bed every five years. Five years is about all I can stand of Hartman's suggestions for fine-tuning the radio. And five years is all he can stand of my suggestions about setting the alarm for different times on different mornings.

I can set the alarm but cannot tune a radio. Hartman can set the radio but cannot tune an alarm. There is an important lesson here about our differing and possibly complementary abilities, but I don't have time to think about it now.

Unfortunately our old radio alarm clock gave out while it was on Hartman's side of the bed. I read all 12 pages of directions at least a dozen times, and reviewed them each evening before giving instructions to Hartman, the radio operator on the radio alarm side of the bed. We have lovely music, right on station in full stereo, but we have yet to get up on time. Some mornings we haven't gotten up at all.

There are five bars on top of the radio which go up and down. They are variously labelled "snooze", "radio-alarm", "auto-manual", "off-power", "bright-dim".

There are, in addition to the five bars, five

knobs and four buttons on the face of the clock radio. As I understand it, the five knobs operate the radio somehow. But I don't need to know anything about them for another four years. Even then I won't need to know much because Hartman is not bashful about telling me what I can do with the knobs.

My concern, then, is with the four buttons on the front which are labelled "sleep", "time", "alarm", and "slow". I am also concerned with the five bars on top. In order to set the clock, push "time" and "fast". Do not push fast too long or it will rush past the proper time. In which case you will have to push time and fast through the next 24 hours. There is something to be said for clocks which just repeat the same twelve numbers day and night.

The slow button is the one to push as the clock digits approach the proper time. It advances the digits with more deliberation and chances are you can stop before pushing things too far.

Once the clock is set, the alarm must be set. Push the alarm and the fast button. Go through the exercise as before in setting the clock, stop fast and push slow as the proper minute appears on the clock.

In order to have the radio turn on in the morning, place bars two and three up or down, and bar four in the opposite position. I think. It doesn't matter one way or another about bar five. If you want the radio to play before you go to sleep, push sleep. Nine times out of ten, nothing happens. In which case, push sleep and slow. The radio will then play 59 through 00 minutes. The longer you push ´slow´ the shorter the time the radio will play. To turn the radio off, do not push the "off-power" bar. That would be too logical. Instead, push "snooze" except in the morning when you push "bright."

Obviously the operating instructions for our new radio alarm clock are complex. Hartman has gallantly offered to give up his turn and let me have the clock on my side of the bed right now. But until I can master the four buttons and five bars, I cannot bear to face five knobs.

So for another four years we are fated to have these difficult conversations about how to set the dumb thing just before going to sleep. It is just one more of the many trials and tribulations encountered in marriages of long standing. Fortunately, there are countering joys.

33. Shifting

I have a new car. It has a stick shift with eight speeds forward—if you count power and economy—and one or two in reverse. I´m not sure about the reverse speeds. I don´t know if it is possible or even desireable to back up in power or not. I´ve been inclined to back up in economy only, so far.

When I got the car, our grown children, one after the other, asked if I could shift for myself. They have forgotten, all of them, just who it was who sat in the suicide seat, silently screaming, when they were practicing their second shifting lesson in the church parking lot.

Their father, Hartman, gave each one of them their first shifting lesson, then turned them over to me. He used to do things like that a lot. He would pronounce sentence on one of them for some misdeed, and say, "You cannot go outside to play for the rest of the day," then off he would go for a frolicsome day at the office and leave me stuck in the house with the grouchy culprit.

But I have forgiven him for all that, and for anything else he may ever do or say because he has given me this neat little car. Which I can shift. I learned to shift when I learned to drive at the age of twelve.

Of course, cars were different back when I was twelve. Second gear was in first place, first in second, third where it is now, and reverse in place of the present fourth gear position.

Shifting, like riding a bike, is something you never forget. This may be why I have a tendency to jerk forward and stall every time I try to back up. I haven't been able to forget reverse position which is now fourth gear.

Up to now I have personally driven the car 87 miles. They have not been easy miles for I am one of those persons who cannot chew gum and walk at the same time. Furthermore, I never fail to panic in a pinch.

When I turn a corner, put on the turn indicator, clutch, brake, accelerate, shift down to second, then maybe to first, and perhaps, in case of a steep hill such as the one we ascend every time we come home, shift to power besides, I really panic. Fortunately I don't smoke. If I had a cigarette to do something with during those frantic moments, everyone in the general neighborhood would have to break for shelter.

I'm not smooth at starting out either. Only this morning Hartman rode into town with me. "I'm glad I don't have a hat on," he observed. "It would have just popped off into the back seat."

Rounding corners is also exciting; I try to stay above 15 miles an hour so I won't have to shift down. I feel it is bad for the car to have to change gears all the time.

In spite of all these minor problems, I CAN shift, as I told the children. I survived a run down 28th Street in Grand Rapids one day when I found myself caught in the daily five o'clock Roman chariot race. It was white knuckles, hunched shoulder, clenched teeth and sheer terror all the way as I had to shift down, shift up, clutch, break, accelerate, steer and watch out for the hordes of crazy drivers. My blood raced when I glanced into the rear view mirror and saw a truck bumper coming at me at eye level.

I have survived even the traffic light in Fremont where those try their tricks who find 28th Street too tame. I approach the intersection all attention, blood racing, body tense, gears shifting. If you some time recognize me at that light, understand the situation, for goodness' sakes. Don't expect me, on top of everything else, to wave at you. Or even to smile.

I don't know why you wouldn't recognize me. Hartman, who gave me the car, thoughtfully placed a name plate which says 'Nancy' on the front of it. After this piece appears in print, the name plate might as well be a sandwich board, mounted on top of the car as they do in England, with a giant red L for Learner painted on both sides.

But I appreciate Hartman's confidence in my ability to learn. Learn I will. When I've gone another 87 miles and am good enough to enter the beginner's class, I'm going to ask one of our grown children to give me a lesson or two in the church parking lot.

34. Choco...
Choco...
Chocolate

According to an article in Time Magazine, chocolate is a $3.4 Billion annual business in the U.S. The consumption of chocolate is more than 9 pounds per capita a year. Some U.S. citizens don't eat chocolate at all; others among us have such a passion for the stuff we eat more than 9 pounds a year and make up for those who don't.

As a certified chocoloholic, I can tell you more about chocolate and about eating it than you want to know I admit that I have secretly purchased family-size packages of Reeses peanutbutter cups and eaten the entire contents on the way home from the grocery store. I have made a batch of double chocolate brownies for the family dessert and then promptly sat down to consume the whole thing myself before anybody showed up. If there is chocolate within 50 feet, I can't rest until I have eaten it. I can't even talk about it without being overcome with a terrible yen.

I had to prepare myself for writing this piece about chocolate by eating two pieces of the XXX chocolate cake which is wrapped in foil and tucked away in the bottom of the freezer. I can't tell you anything else that is in the freezer, but I'll be aware that the cake is there until the last piece is gone.

Right now I'm writing very fast in order to finish this article before the chocolate "high" wears off.

Chocolate is made from a blend of cocoa beans found in pods which grow right out of the trunk of the cocoa tree. Inexpensive chocolates are made from inferior cocoa beans, extended with paraffin, and mixed with preservatives to lengthen shelf life. In the case of filled candies, the outside layer of chocolate is very thin and is sprayed on.

Expensive chocolates, on the other hand, are made from hand-picked cocoa beans which are carefully prepared and blended without paraffin extenders or preservatives. The filled chocolates are hand-dipped several times to make a thick coating of chocolate. Naturally, I like expensive chocolates best.

It is one of the miracles of nature that a little half-ounce piece of chocolate can be transformed into a full pound of avoirdupois overnight. And as far as I'm concerned, a little half-ounce piece of chocolate is not enough. I have had to refuse a sample of the finest Belgian Cote d'Or because one piece would only drive me mad.

Such an appetite for chocolate leads to terminal obesity. Lately I have been forced by the consequences of eating too much chocolate to limit my intake to nothing but the best. In this way, I price myself out of the habit, so to speak. When I can afford it—fortunately, not too often—I eat Hershey's Golden Almond bars, Lady Godiva chocolates, Sweetland Candy Shoppee special order chocolate covered almonds, and other special kinds on which I will not dwell any further. I may drool into my typewriter and rust the type bars.

The local demand for chocolate reflects the

national market. According to the grocery manager of Valueland, the chocolate section of the candy department does 'phenomenal' business. Chocolate candy placed in a bargain bin near the checkout counters is an immediate sellout even when only slightly marked down.

The Ben Franklin Store has augmented its candy bar business with a stock of Wilton candy-making supplies. Candy molds, foil cups, cookbooks, gift boxes, and bulk chocolate prove to be popular items for those who have the will power to make their own. I can't make candy myself because I can't wait for the chocolate to harden.

Hartsema's newsstand is the only place in Fremont at present where good chocolates are sold by the box. Quality chocolates have a shelf life of less than three months. But keeping the supply fresh isn't a problem at the newsstand which grosses nearly $40,000 a year on the 4 foot by 6 foot display counter of Russell Stovers candies at the front of the store.

My own candy consumption is augmented now and then with a dessert made, perhaps, from one of the marvelous recipes in Maida Heatter's "Book of Great Chocolate Desserts." There are several other cook books dealing only with chocolate which have been published recently; a reflection on the chocolate craze of the times.

Or it may be just another way the publishers have of keeping diet books on the best seller list. Today their customers will buy a chocolate cookbook, the publishers say to themselves, as they rub their hands in glee, "Next week it will be a book on diets."

Superb baking chocolate as well as fine candies

and special blends of bulk chocolate for candy making and baking can be ordered from several sources which issue catalogs. I don't order chocolates by mail very often either. Just the appearance of the catalog in the mailbox is enough to make me put on 5 pounds.

Although I have hardly scratched the surface of my passion for chocolate, I can't dwell upon it anymore. I would go downtown this very minute and buy a box of Russel Stovers candy but I can't find my purse.

I know precisely where I hid four Hershey's Golden Almond bars three weeks ago,—there is half of one left— but I can't remember where I put my purse this morning.

Hartman has suggested that I should keep a chocolate bar in my purse. Then I would know exactly where it was all the time.

35. The Art of Photography

Photography is a form of art with an ever increasing appeal. For a time, I fancied myself as something of a photographer too. I took pictures of our grandchildren mostly, or of my traveling companion, Hartman, posed smiling in front of some scenic view. I used to imagine that some of my pictures might be considered art by a discerning eye if I would only do something with them. But that was before I ran into the tulips.

Several years ago I picked five tulips, stuck them into a mustard crock and put them on the table. They moved themselves about as cut tulips do; in a slow motion ballet, arranging themselves so gracefully I marvelled at their beauty. But by the time I got around to taking a picture, the tulips were gone, not only from the mustard crock but from the garden as well.

I'm not a candid photographer. When I finally took the picture of our grandson blowing out the candle on his first birthday cake, he was two years old.

Moments with grandchildren are hard to recapture, but I had a chance to try the tulips again when they came up the next year. Placed in the same mustard crock, they arranged themselves as gracefully as before. I put them on a low table, waited until the sun caught them just right and took the picture. Twelve times. A still life arrangement, I thought. Art.

I followed this flurry of photographic activity by a year of careful consideration during which I selected the best of the twelve negatives and had a large print made. The print cost $25.

For the next six months I kept the print on a shelf in the closet with several other things I was sorry I´d done. I needed six months to get over feeling guilty for paying $25 for one of my own prints. Every now and then I would take the print out to look at it and make sure I thought it still looked good.

At last it seemed to be time to take the tulips down to the frame shop to select a suitable frame. No easy task. Should it be of metal or of wood? Plain or ornate? What kind of a mat did it need? Could I stand another six months of guilt over how much the frame was going to cost?

After several trips to the frame shop I settled on a gilt frame with a few dust catching details and a mat which picked up the color of the tulip leaves.

Many weeks later--the mat had to be handwoven in Taiwan or some such nonsense--the picture was framed and I brought it guiltily home and hung it on the wall.

It was wrong. All wrong. It´s the mat, I thought. Tulip green matting doesn´t look right anywhere. Suddenly the guilt I´d been planning to harbor for the next six months vanished completely. Suddenly I found myself thinking price was no object where Art is concerned. And these tulips were Art.

I took the picture back to the frame shop to be re-matted with a natural linen which the shop keeper had in stock. This time, I thought, when I

I saw the re-framed print, the tulips would look perfect no matter where they were hung. And I hung them on four different walls before I was satisfied. More than twenty years ago Hartman and I fought our last battle over how many holes one can pound in a wall. I try not to abuse the privilege that I won at that time--a person can pound as many holes as she needs--but this was Art.

Satisfied at length that the tulips were hung to their greatest advantage, I led Hartman in to view the finished work. He looked at it for the skip of a heartbeat and said: "Those tulips are too close to the top of the picture."

He's right, of course. Now whenever I look at that picture, I don't see the lovely still life arrangement in the mustard crock, the gilt frame which looks so perfect on the wall, or the linen matting which is just right; I see those dumb tulips too close to the top.

36. On Ice

Winter driving can be hazardous to your health as anyone who lives in Michigan can testify. One simply cannot go through a typical winter in this state without being caught out in a blizzard, on ice-covered roads, or at least once battling impassable snowdrifts. It makes good conversation afterwards but it is no fun at the time.

A few years ago we moved to the top of a hill. The driveway we share with the neighbors is not only up hill, it is a quarter of a mile long and has a 90 degree curve. Going up the driveway in typical winter conditions is a thrill.

The first storm of the season arrived the day before Christmas the year we moved in. Ice covered the driveway and I couldn't get the car up the hill. I had to walk. Walking the last quarter mile home became common practice that year.

The first time it happened Hartman jumped into his vehicle and drove down the hill to rescue me. He hooked a chain onto my car, climbed into his own car, stepped on the gas...and slip back into my grill.

He spent Christmas eve and much of Christmas day pounding the grill back into shape. We no longer had small children at home to put toys together for and I suppose he had to have something to do with his hands.

Another time deep snow rather than ice prevented my ascent. Hartman had by now equipped himself with a four-wheel drive vehicle which gave him greater control during a hazard.

He has had no confidence in my driving since the time I drove full speed into the back of his car while I was waving at the neighbors during a push-the-stalled car drama we enacted years ago when we lived on Pine Street. This is why at the outset of the episode I´m about to relate, he told me not to touch anything.

"Pay attention to what we are trying to do," he said, speaking slowly as one might to someone who is dull-witted. "Don´t touch anything. Just sit in the car and steer. I´ll pull the car up the hill."

I followed his instructions to the letter. I didn´t even turn on the ignition. When we reached the 90 degree curve, he went around the curve in his 4-wheel drive vehicle, and I went straight ahead into the snowbank. Of course, since I had not turned on the ignition, the steering wheel was locked in place.

On another occasion, he was plowing snow off the driveway with a small garden tractor. The job was too big for the equipment and the tractor stalled at the bottom of the drive.

This time I was assigned a position in the lead car. He sat on the tractor and watched in sheer horror as I laid a patch starting up the hill.

Fortunately, I heard his cry and stopped before the chain between us stretched tight. He would have been catapulted right into Second Lake.

He claims I did it on purpose in a moment of pique. But I didn´t. Without Hartman, what would

I write about now that the children have fled? It happened because automatic shift cars race when cold and my car was cold.

A cold automatic shift car has gotten me into trouble going down the hill too. Until I hit upon the idea of shifting into neutral and coasting down, I often ended up among the pine trees on the 90 degree curve. Or what was worse, gliding down the ice with brakes on, wheels sliding, toward Ramshorn road, hoping something would grab before I hurtled out into the oncoming traffic.

After several exciting winters on the driveway, my problems were solved by the proper kind of car; one with eight speeds forward and front wheel drive. My little car makes it up and down hill in safety every time. So far.

But drama on the driveway goes on. The neighbors have taken up where I left off. When they go down the hill, they still have to wonder if they'll ever get up. When they head home on a winter day, they lean forward, clench their teeth, grip the steering wheel, and race up Ramshorn road to make a running start, just as I used to do.

Sometimes they succeed, and as we come up the hill after them we see their swerving tracks. Sometimes they make it half way up and hang there, spinning wheels. Sometimes they try and try again, sliding, finally, back into the ditch.

When that happens, Hartman goes down in his 4-wheel drive to pull them up as he did for me so many times. Then I may lend my substantial weight to the rear wheels of the stuck car by sitting on the trunk. But usually I just take a position on an overlooking snowbank and empathize. There, but for my front wheel drive, spin I.

37. Burnt Crisp

We have an old family recipe handed down through at least three generations which is called Burnt Crisp. My mother used to serve it as a side dish, an accompaniment to whatever was her second choice for the main course. Scrambled eggs, usually. My mother was very quick to laugh and she always served her Burnt Crisp with a generous dollop of laughter.

She happened on the recipe because my father never came home for meals on time the way other fathers did. She would sit on our front porch and watch Mr. Branstrom or Mr. Murphy walk by on their way home at 12 noon or 6 sharp and wonder at length why, oh why, did her own husband never look at the clock.

Meanwhile she had three whining children to placate and smoke billowing out of the kitchen at the back of the house. My sister and I still whine when we get hungry.

My own Burnt Crisp was usually made with vegetables. When the children were young I would put the vegetables on the stove to boil and then forget them entirely, for I had to turn total attention to whatever emergency came up. In a family of four children there is no end to the supply of emergencies coming up. When I thought of the vegetables again, they would have boiled dry and be in smoke if not in flame. That is my version of Burnt Crisp.

I always served the vegetables anyway, garnishing them with either laughter or tears, depending upon the nature of the emergency which produced the Burnt Crisp in the first place. Even when vegetables were done to a turn, the children would refuse to eat them, so why not give them something that deserved to be spurned?

I forgot about Burnt Crisp after the children left and the microwave came. I now cook vegetables in the microwave oven. They turn out rubbery sometimes but they never burn to a crisp. If I do burn something that I'm cooking--it doesn't always take an emergency to divert my attention--we can always eat out. We do eat out, in fact. Often.

Then, recently, we had dinner at the home of one of the children. Although she had never asked for the recipe--and I had never offered it--she had the making of Burnt Crisp down to perfection.

Her Burnt Crisp had started out as lasagna. When it came out of the oven her response was exactly according to the family recipe. She had the surprised expression, the hesitation--while she made up her mind whether to serve it with laughter or tears--and then the laughter just right. She carried the offering into the living room to display it to the other guests.

"Ah, Brownies!" her father said.

She is a true descendent of a grandmother she never knew; quick to laugh. Burnt Crisp tastes better served with a laugh.

38. Small Town

A friend who travels the banquet circuit told me she was seated next to a young woman from Los Angeles not long ago, and sometime between the fruit cup and the Swiss steak the young woman turned on her, looked down her nose which was—presumably--long, and said: "What on earth do you find to do in a wide spot in the road like Fremont?" Fortunately my friend has a ready wit. There is no apparent connection between my brain and my tongue and if that question had been addressed to me, I wouldn't have been able to think of a thing to say until the next day.

My friend told her dining companion that we do things in Fremont that people do everywhere, only we enjoy them more. We play tennis without waiting for a court and golf without reserving tee time. We cross-country ski, hike, boat, dance, hunt, fish, and swim in our own neighborhood.

We live only fifty miles by quiet country roads from the very cultural center of the midwest, she went on, slightly carried away. She meant Grand Rapids, and must be forgiven the exaggeration. When your back is to the wall you have to fight with all the ammunition you can muster. Never mind if some of the bullets are blanks.

We dine out, she said, play cards, pursue our work and our hobbies without fighting traffic, pushing crowds, or breathing smog. Our school system is excellent, our citizens concerned. We know people not in quantity, perhaps, but we know them in depth.

She defended small towns beautifully, and if someone ever says something like that to me, I'll send my friend around to give them a speech.

But there are a few peculiarities of small town life which those of us who live here take for granted. A cousin of mine reported that when he drove into Fremont early one Sunday morning after twenty years out in the big, big world, he thought the whole town had been evacuated.

Fortunately, a flutter of movement caught his eye as he passed the newsstand. He stopped and went in, relieved to find someone to ask what had happened. It was, he had long ago forgotten, the usual Sunday morning scene.

So. When two young women who were born and raised in Chicago were to be our weekend guests, Hartman and I thought it would be helpful to warn them in advance. Neither one of them had ever spent more than five minutes in a town the size of Fremont. Five minutes is the time it takes to drive from the Fremont city limits west to the city limits east. Except on Saturdays when the traffic is heavy and it may take six minutes.

Do not be deceived, we told them, by the light flow of traffic on Main Street. Driving in downtown Fremont is dangerous. Local jay walkers are skittish. Those few pedestrians who actually cross the street at the traffic light do not understand the signal system. They know they are supposed to do something when the light changes, but they're never sure just what. We know you have solved the pedestrian problem in Chicago, we said,--traffic lights say "walk" or "don´t walk" at the appropriate times, and jay-walkers are killed--but no one has suggested such drastic measures here.

Local drivers do not keep their eyes on the road. They feel it is more important to see who is downtown than to watch the traffic. A driver I know noticed too late that the car ahead had stopped to back into a parking space while she was driving blithely ahead, waving and nodding like the queen of England to people on the sidewalk. Is it any wonder that the local jay-walkers are skittish?

Most city visitors enjoy the experience of shopping in a small town, we told them. The clerks are helpful and interested and very apt to turn your shopping excursion into a social occasion with an exchange of the news of the day.

The native costume is comfortable and informal. Be prepared for weather that is hot, cold, sunny, dismal, and wet. All on the same day. Bring a warm jacket if you intend to look in on a grocery store. The Shop ´n Save features arctic temperatures year around.

The whistle blows at noon on weekdays and at 3 o´clock on Monday afternoons. It is not a disaster warning. The local residents relax when they hear it and check their clocks.

Any other time the whistle blows it means there is either a tornado or a fire. In either case, get off the street. Volunteer firemen on foot and in cars or pickups equipped with sirens come tearing toward the fire station from all directions.

The number 2 on the Fremont push-button

telephones has a tendency to wear out. If your
call fails to go through, go to a dial phone. The
Fremont prefix is 924. The AT&T representative
told me the 2's wear out because they are used too
often. He did not explain what, if anything
happens to the 9's and the 4's. Nor did he have
any suggestions for avoiding the problem.

Finally, we told them, the sounds you hear
above the breezes morning and evening are birds,
frogs, cicadas, and other forms of wild life. And
the strange fragrance you may catch when you put
your nose to the wind is probably just the fresh
clean air. Enjoy.

39. Age is a Matter of Time

This year's birthday marked another decade in my life and brought me a certain preoccupation with time. I trust the preoccupation is only temporary. I don't feel any older than I ever did. And a person is only as old as she feels, to quote an old saw. Some of you may be too young to know what a 'saw' is: it is an obsolete word for a maxim or proverb.

Nevertheless, I note with interest the ages of the people whose names appear in the obituaries. I collect names of late bloomers in the hope that there may still be some chance for me. I admire extravagantly older people who are still growing in spirit and intellect.

When someone says with an air of tolerant amusement that their 73-year-old mother still bakes her own bread, or has taken up French, I wonder what is so remarkable about that. Now 73 does not seem old anymore.

I no longer wait for habitual late-comers. My time is as dear to me as theirs is to them, I have decided at last. I will give my time away, or even waste it, but I will no longer use it up waiting for Godot or whoever. Godot is a character in a play; he never shows up, so nothing ever happens.

My attitude toward wedding anniversaries has also changed. At one time, when the neighbors celebrated their tenth anniversary, I thought they had been married for eons. They were also making

$5,000 a year and if we ever made that much, we would be rich, rich, rich.

People who celebrated silver anniversaries were, in my view back then, patriarchs of the town. In fact, I marvelled that their children were still young and able enough to put on the anniversary party.

But now I know quite lively people who have been married 50 years. And some of them say even 50 years is not long enough.

Time is unreal. Marked arbitrarily, it seems, by clock and calendars or by phases of the moon, the same span of time is both long and short.

When I was a brand new bride, some time ago and yet just yesterday, I went to a doctor a few days after the wedding for treatment of tonsillitis. He asked me, in the course of my visit, how long I had been married.

It was none of his business, I thought. At my present time of life, I would have told him to mind his manners. At that time, however, twenty-two years old and two days married, I felt compelled to answer in deference to his advanced age. He was probably thirty.

But it would not be necessary, I decided, to tell the total truth. I didn't want him to know I was such a very recent bride. So I lied. I told him I'd been married a long time. "Three weeks," I said.

Or, to repeat another old saw, time is relative.